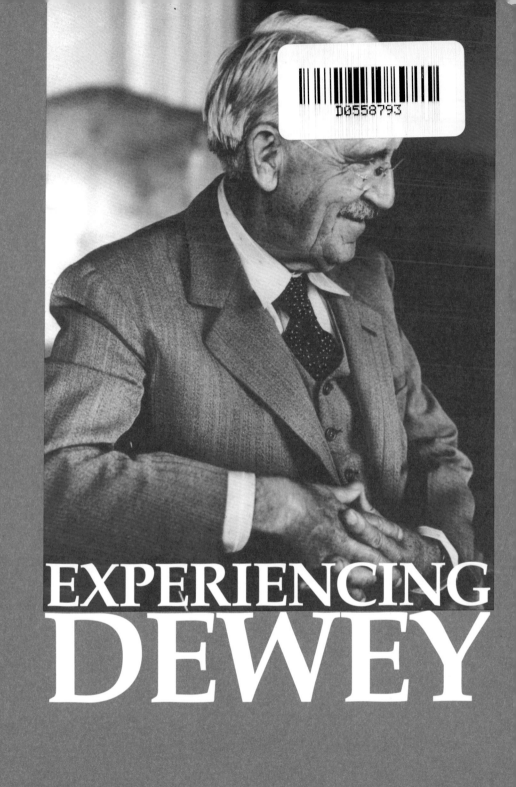

EXPERIENCING
DEWEY

EXPERIENCING DEWEY

INSIGHTS FOR TODAY'S CLASSROOM

*Edited by Donna Adair Breault
and Rick Breault*

With a Foreword by David T. Hansen

Kappa Delta Pi
International Honor Society in Education
Indianapolis, Indiana

Printed in the United States of America
05 06 07 08 09   5 4 3 2 1

Direct all inquiries to the Director of Publications, Kappa Delta Pi, 3707 Woodview Trace, Indianapolis, IN 46268-1158.

Executive Director
Michael P. Wolfe

Director of Publications
Kathie-Jo Arnoff

Editors
Karen L. Allen
Helen McCarthy

Design and Layout
Chuck Jarrell
Cindy Kelley

To order, call Kappa Delta Pi Headquarters (800-284-3167) or visit KDP Online *(www.kdp.org)*. Quantity discounts for more than 20 copies.
KDP Order Code 522

Portraits, photos, and Dewey's personal correspondence that appear in this volume are from the Special Collections Research Center, Morris Library, Southern Illinois University Carbondale. Used with permission.

The photo of Dewey surrounded by children and the postcards are courtesy of Craig Kridel.

Library of Congress Cataloging-in-Publication Data

Experiencing Dewey : insights for today's classroom / edited by Donna Adair Breault and Rick Breault ; with a foreword by David T. Hansen.
        p. cm.
  Includes bibliographical references.
  ISBN 0-912099-42-9 (alk. paper)
  1. Dewey, John, 1859-1952. 2. Education--Philosophy.
  3. Education--Experimental methods. I. Breault, Donna Adair.
II. Breault, Rick.
  LB875.D5E96 2005
  370'.1--dc22
                        2005007771

TABLE OF CONTENTS

Part I: Active Learning

Part II: The Educative Experience

Part III: Critical Thinking

IV: Inquiry and Education

Part V: Democratic Citizenship

Sources for Dewey Quotes

Dewey, J. 1952. Introduction. In *The use of resources in education*, ed. E. R. Clapp, vii–xi. New York: Harper & Row.

Dewey, J. 1972. *The significance of the problem of knowledge*. In *John Dewey: The early works, 1882–1898*, ed. J. A. Boydston, Vol. 5: 1895–1898, 3–24. Carbondale, IL: Southern Illinois University Press.

Dewey, J. 1972. My pedagogic creed. In *John Dewey: The early works, 1882–1898*, ed. J. A. Boydston, Vol. 5: 1895–1898, 84–95. Carbondale, IL: Southern Illinois University Press.

Dewey, J. 1976. *The school and society*. In *John Dewey: The middle works, 1899–1924*, ed. J. A. Boydston, Vol. 1: 1899–1901, 1–112. Carbondale, IL: Southern Illinois University Press.

Dewey, J. 1976. *The child and the curriculum*. In *John Dewey: The middle works, 1899–1924*, ed. J. A. Boydston, Vol. 2: 1902–1903, 271–92. Carbondale, IL: Southern Illinois University Press.

Dewey, J. 1977. Experience and objective idealism. In *John Dewey: The middle works, 1899–1924*, ed. J. A. Boydston, Vol. 3: 1903–1906, 128–44. Carbondale, IL: Southern Illinois University Press.

Dewey, J. 1977. The relation of theory to practice in education. In *John Dewey: The middle works, 1899–1924*, ed. J. A. Boydston, Vol. 3: 1903–1906, 249–72. Carbondale, IL: Southern Illinois University Press.

Dewey, J. 1978. *How we think*. In *John Dewey: The middle works, 1899–1924*, ed. J. A. Boydston, Vol. 6: 1910–1911, 177–356. Carbondale, IL: Southern Illinois University Press.

Dewey, J. 1980. *Democracy and education*. In *John Dewey: The middle works, 1899–1924*, ed. J. A. Boydston, Vol. 9: 1916, 1–402. Carbondale, IL: Southern Illinois University Press.

Dewey, J. 1984. *The quest for certainty: A study of the relation of knowledge and action*. In *John Dewey: The later works, 1925–1953*, ed. J. A. Boydston, Vol. 4: 1929, 1–250. Carbondale, IL: Southern Illinois University Press.

Dewey, J. 1984. *The sources of a science of education*. In *John Dewey: The later works, 1925–1953*, ed. J. A. Boydston, Vol. 5: 1929–1930, 1–40. Carbondale, IL: Southern Illinois University Press.

Dewey, J. 1986. *A common faith*. In *John Dewey: The later works, 1925–1953*, ed. J. A. Boydston, Vol. 9: 1933–1934, 1–60. Carbondale, IL: Southern Illinois University Press.

Dewey, J. 1987. *Art as experience*. In *John Dewey: The later works, 1925–1953*, ed. J. A. Boydston, Vol. 10: 1934, 1–456. Carbondale, IL: Southern Illinois University Press.

Dewey, J. 1987. Democracy and educational administration. In *John Dewey: The later works, 1925–1953*, ed. J. A. Boydston, Vol. 11: 1935–1937, 217–25. Carbondale, IL: Southern Illinois University Press.

Dewey, J. 1987. Education and social change. In *John Dewey: The later works, 1925–1953*, ed. J. A. Boydston, Vol. 11: 1935–1937, 408–20. Carbondale, IL: Southern Illinois University Press.

Dewey, J. 1988. *Experience and education.* In *John Dewey: The later works, 1925–1953*, ed. J. A. Boydston, Vol. 13: 1938–1939, 1–62. Carbondale, IL: Southern Illinois University Press.

Dewey, J. 1988. Creative democracy: The task before us. In *John Dewey: The later works, 1925–1953*, ed. J. A. Boydston, Vol. 14: 1939–1941, 224–30. Carbondale, IL: Southern Illinois University Press.

Foreword

Reflection on education is as old as democratic thinking. So are forces that would undermine education and put it at the service of narrow interests. Educational thought and practice, and their many counterfeits, sprang from democratic experiments undertaken by the Greeks 2,500 years ago. John Dewey was intimately familiar with those experiments. His favorite reading during his long and illustrious life as a philosopher and educator was Plato. Dewey appreciated how the Greeks had forced to the front the distinction between socialization and education. The former involves cultural reproduction and will be necessary as long as human life endures—consider, for example, the need to learn language. But education means questioning, inquiring, judging, and more. That fact accounts for why education has for centuries been a source both of fear (think of the mindset of totalitarians) and of boundless hope.

Teachers work at the crossroads of socialization and education. They are responsible for passing along important knowledge, skills, and understandings without which society cannot maintain itself. However, especially in a democratic society, teachers have a unique opportunity to engage in educational work. They can help their students learn to think independently, to understand the values of argument and evidence, to weigh contrasting views on an issue, and to appreciate differences in experience and outlook. This opportunity converts teaching into a genuine adventure, for the teacher as much as for students. Many educators have argued that to participate in the adventure—and, above all, to sustain it in the face of the many pressures that work against it—teachers need to reflect about the meaning of their work rather than just about what they do. Educators also have argued that teachers need to talk about teaching with like-minded peers and associates, regardless of the level of the system where they work. In this way, teaching endures as a human practice. It stays alive and healthy through an ongoing conversation among teachers in which all can participate, whether novice or experienced.

This book can help fuel the conversation. It contains many familiar and admired quotes from Dewey's wide-ranging corpus of writing (his complete works have been published in 37 volumes). Each quote is followed by brief commentary, mostly by university-based teachers, but also by teachers serving in the nation's schools. The commentators do not always see eye-to-eye with one another, nor will readers agree with all they have to say. I believe that readers will find the quotes and the commentary provocative and a stimulus to their own thinking. Just as the structure of the book—Dewey's voice followed by that of a commentator—mirrors the very idea of a conversation, so readers of the book can "converse" in their own ways about what they discover. I urge readers to follow the example of the commentators by responding themselves to the quotes from Dewey. That adventure promises to be enlightening and enjoyable. I also urge readers to move from the quotes to the original texts from which they come.

It is particularly valuable to read these texts in company with other people. See for yourself why, for 100 years and more, countless educators in the United States and elsewhere have found inspiration, guidance, and profound insight in Dewey's writing. Keep the conversation on teaching going.

David T. Hansen
President, The John Dewey Society
Teachers College, Columbia University
New York City, March 18, 2004

The editors and publisher would like to thank the following education professionals, all leaders in Kappa Delta Pi, for reading and critically analyzing early drafts of the chapters.

Lisa Goeken-Galliart
Illinois State University
Normal, Illinois

Valeri R. Helterbran
Indiana University of Pennsylvania
Indiana, Pennsylvania

J. Wesley Null
The University of Texas–Austin
Austin, Texas

Maria Stallions
Barry University
Miami Shores, Florida

Introduction

Rick Breault and Donna Adair Breault

John Dewey is more than a scholarly influence in our household. In fact, you might say that he always has been part of our day-to-day living—and not just a part of our preparation for some future life. Rick's first publication was a short piece reflecting on the 70th anniversary of *Democracy and Education*. We met at a conference when each of us went to hear the other's paper on Dewey and Freire. Some of our friends might even recall the holiday greeting cards that featured J.D. wearing a Santa Claus cap and expressing the hope that the receiver would *"experience* a happy holiday." If you were to talk to any of Donna's graduate students, they likely would recount the missionary zeal with which they were introduced to *How We Think* and may still wonder whether we based our wedding vows on *My Pedagogic Creed.* In a way, you could say that the idea for this collection was conceived as a sort of evangelical effort.

Over the years, as we have introduced Dewey's writings to both undergraduate and graduate students, we have tried to elicit reactions on the scale of Oliver Wendell Holmes's (1941, 287) famous remark about Dewey's writing:

> It seemed to me . . . to have a feeling of intimacy with the inside of the
> cosmos that I found unequaled. So methought God would have spoken
> had he been inarticulate but keenly desirous to tell you how it was.

Our students wade through the often dense sentence structure and are confused as to whether Dewey was describing a position with which he disagreed or one that he espoused. Then, every once in a while, they come to a few sentences that knock them off their pedagogical feet; and they can never look at their teaching the same way again. Time after time, when students have been ready to quit, we have encouraged them to continue reading just a few more paragraphs so that they might find that it somehow all comes together. And usually it does.

That approach has worked well, as far as it goes. However, for the reader who has not yet become a true believer and may not be reading in a class setting, that type of mentally exhausting and sometimes frustrating initial exposure to Dewey's writing may not be the spark that sends that individual into the rest of the philosopher's enormous body of work. Moreover, we are not sure that the best way to win converts to Dewey's thought is to send readers diving headlong and unassisted into *Experience and Nature, Logic: The Theory of Inquiry,* or *The Influence of Darwin on Philosophy.* Still, there are gems to be mined even from the most difficult volumes.

Beyond the intellectual challenges and rewards of reading Dewey, there is another dimension. It is difficult to walk away from his work unmoved—especially his writing about schools and teaching. To engage seriously with Dewey's work is to be motivated, encouraged, reenergized, and overwhelmed with the possibilities of an active, inquiring classroom. If you truly have entered his world,

1

you cannot avoid making a decision. You either can ignore what you found there and continue teaching like you always have; or you can live with the knowledge that you are somehow less of a teacher than you can and should be.

Dewey, the Person

One last dimension of Dewey has come to be more important in our own teaching and reading in recent years. That has to do with Dewey, the person. Several years ago, we were fortunate enough to see Craig Kridel's slides of Dewey playing at the beach and just having fun with children. Knowing about that part of his life, his practical work with schools, and his commitment to a lived philosophy, we doubt that he would have been happy knowing that the discussion of his work, more often than not, is limited to scholarly circles, theoretical debates, or simplistic historical overviews of the progressive movement in foundations textbooks. We would like to believe that Dewey would feel more honored and perhaps even more excited by the story of a teacher who began teaching *according* to his work than by news of another class or American Educational Research Association panel *about* his work.

Our notions about Dewey as a person came together as an outgrowth of what was originally a humorous aside during a conversation about popularizing Dewey. One of us suggested that what Deweyan disciples needed was the sort of daily devotion book common in various Christian traditions. Typically, those books offer a passage from scripture followed by a short written reflection or meditation on the ideas in the scripture. Because we often had joked about quoting from the writings of "St. John," the suggestion was in keeping with our common faith in progressive education. But soon, the discussion turned serious. Maybe a book like that really could be a meaningful and useful way to embody our desire to more effectively introduce educators to the broad scope of Dewey's works and to do so in a personal and practical way. Furthermore, maybe such a collection also could prove valuable to experienced Deweyan readers and thinkers by rekindling the personal and pedagogical engagement that led to their initial attachment to the philosopher.

About the Collection of Essays

The process of actually constructing this volume has been a truly enjoyable and fulfilling one. Though we anticipated that bringing this dream to fruition would be rewarding, the task was even more meaningful in that we learned so much and enjoyed the help of so many friends. In identifying quotations for possible inclusion, we unearthed some Deweyan gems that we had never noticed before and were reminded once again of the enormous breadth of Dewey's genius. Then, after selecting hundreds of quotations, we began the process of inviting potential authors, asking them to select a quotation (or suggest one of their own) and reflect on its importance to them. The response we received was encouraging in many ways. Of course, we truly were honored to be able to include contributions from scholars whose reputations in our field are without question.

We also were thankful for the words of encouragement and support we received from those same people, who saw this as a labor of love and an opportunity to revisit familiar quotations from a new perspective. More than one contributor mentioned that this short piece was the most difficult they had written in a long time, for we had asked all the contributors to step away from their traditional roles of scholars and interpreters of Dewey. Instead, we asked them to draw from their personal and emotional encounter with Dewey's work—an exercise that is often difficult for those of us trained in and rewarded for traditional scholarship.

While you will find many of the names in this collection familiar, many you will not. It was important to us to include the voices of teachers, administrators, and students who probably would not consider themselves to be Deweyan scholars but who have nonetheless been affected by Dewey's writing. That is the spirit in which we hope this book will be read. Despite Dewey's obviously formidable intellect and his sometimes heated engagement with the scholars of his day, ultimately, we believe that Dewey wanted his philosophy to be lived by those who work in schools. He wanted his ideas to be used to create humane, vibrant classrooms. This aspect of his work, we envisioned, could be represented best by those who have been revitalized through their introduction to some aspect of his philosophy and are still immersed in the day-to-day work of the classroom teacher.

How To Use This Book

The approach taken in this book is not, however, without its risks. Whenever words are taken out of context, something important can be lost or, worse yet, misinterpreted. All the authors have made an attempt to recontextualize the quotes to the extent possible, and we deem all the contributions to be true to the intent and content of the original sources. The other risk, which is even more difficult to avoid, is that some readers—especially those previously unfamiliar with Dewey—could come away thinking that they have gained a sense of Dewey's work and are ready to either reject it or use it in their teaching in a way that captures only the most superficial essence of his thought. It is not our intention to promote the kind of simplistic "learning by doing" misuse of progressive educational philosophy that led to so many attacks on the movement and to the need for Dewey to disavow some aspects of the movement and defend his own ideas in his later work.

We strongly encourage those of you who are new to Dewey's work to read the full works from which the quotations are drawn. For the sake of consistency throughout the text, all the quotations are cited from the pages on which they are found in *The Collected Works of John Dewey, 1882–1953*. However, we also have provided the names of the original books, papers, letters, or articles for those of you who want to find individual copies of those sources to begin your further reading.

How This Book Is Organized

Experiencing Dewey is organized into what are arguably five of the central ideas in Dewey's educational thought. In Part I, "Active Learning," the authors reflect on what might be the most commonly misunderstood or oversimplified aspect of Dewey's work. You will find that Dewey, who never actually used the phrase "learning by doing," intended something very challenging and substantive when he encouraged teachers to get their students actively engaged in their own learning. Similarly, Part II, titled "The Educative Experience," uses Dewey's words and our contributors' reflections to reemphasize the fact that not every experience had by a learner can be considered meaningful and productive.

"Critical Thinking" is the theme of Part III. It also might be considered central to all aspects of a Deweyan education—and maybe to Deweyan thought in general. As Dewey (1978, 232) reminded us:

> *Genuine freedom . . . rests in the trained power of thought, in the ability to 'turn things over,' to look at matters deliberately. . . . If a man's actions are not guided by thoughtful conclusions, then they are guided by inconsiderate impulse, unbalanced appetite . . . or the circumstances of the moment. To cultivate unhindered, unreflective external activity is to foster enslavement. . . . There is probably no more crucial task before teachers than to nurture critical thinking in their students in the face of anti-intellectualism and what often seems to be an overwhelming emphasis on simple recall.*

Too often, however, critical thinking has been misconceived as a set of discrete, teachable skills. Witness the various "critical thinking curricula."

In Part IV, "Inquiry and Education," contributors attempt to recapture the breadth and complexity of the process of critical thinking by resituating it in the process of inquiry. We think that you will find the quotations they have chosen to be especially inspirational. In reading both Dewey's words and the reflections on those words, you will be able to sense some of the excitement that the teachers in Dewey's lab school must have felt as they and their students carried out inquiry that was simultaneously artistic, challenging, freeing, and maybe even a little utopian in its feel.

Ultimately, to understand and find the full meaning of Dewey's work, you must place it in the context of implications for living as a citizen in a democracy. If your only exposure to John Dewey was a few paragraphs in an undergraduate educational foundations text or those ever-popular references to "learning by doing" in a methods course, you might be quite surprised by what you read in the final part, "Democratic Citizenship." Yes, Dewey was concerned with the development of the individual, the mind, and the more meaningful learning of subject matter. But, in the end, what mattered for Dewey is how an individual would live in community with other individuals. In Dewey's (1986, 57) words: "The things in civilization we most prize are not of ourselves. They exist by grace of the doings and sufferings of the continuous human community in which we are a link."

We hope that Dewey would look favorably on this collection and its potential to forge another link in that human community. We also hope that you will read it in that spirit—the spirit of connection. We feel that we have done our part by linking the works of Dewey with teacher-scholars who have formed their own meaningful connections to the philosopher. They, in turn, have acted as the connection through which you may develop a closer link with Dewey. Finally, it will be up to you to translate these ideas into a new set of beliefs, reformed pedagogy, and enlivened conversations with colleagues that might create the connection Dewey would have liked best of all—the connection that brings to fruition the kind of meaningful educational experience he desired for all children.

References

Dewey, J. 1978. *How we think*. In *John Dewey: The middle works, 1899–1924*, ed. J. A. Boydston, Vol. 6: 1910–1911, 177–356. Carbondale, IL: Southern Illinois University Press.

Dewey, J. 1986. *A common faith*. In *John Dewey: The later works, 1925–1953*, ed. J. A. Boydston, Vol. 9: 1933–1934, 1–60. Carbondale, IL: Southern Illinois University Press.

Holmes, O. W. 1941. Letter to Frederick Pollock, 15 May 1931. In *Holmes-Pollock letters: The correspondence of Mr. Justice Holmes and Sir Frederick Pollock 1874–1932*, Vol. 2, ed. M. D. Howe, 287. Cambridge, MA: Harvard University Press.

— ∽ —

PART I
ACTIVE
LEARNING

Active Learning: A Growth Experience

Rick Breault

Few Deweyan concepts have been as misunderstood and misused as the notion of *active learning*. Dewey (1980, 47) conceived active learning as natural to the child:

> *We do not have to draw out or educe positive activities from a child....*
> *Where there is life, there are already eager and impassioned activities.*

Yet, many teachers and teacher educators fail to grasp the complexity and intention required to create learning opportunities that are educative as well as active. Active learning never was meant to let children do whatever they want and follow whatever grabs their attention at the moment. Instead, the task of the educator, as Dewey (1980, 204) explained, is to:

> *engage pupils in these activities in such ways that while manual skill and technical efficiency are gained and immediate satisfaction found in the work, together with preparation for later usefulness, these things shall be subordinated to* education [author's emphasis]*—that is, to intellectual results and the forming of a socialized disposition.*

Beware of Quick-Fix Solutions

Educators today, as were those in Dewey's era, are susceptible to quick-fix solutions and techniques. Look around and we see educational entrepreneurs (a.k.a. "consultants"), and even a few major professional organizations and journals, touting simplistic techniques based on "constructivism" or "multiple intelligences" that seem increasingly far removed from the theories upon which they are based. Well-intentioned teachers—and teacher educators—are excited to find such relatively easy, theory-based, teaching methods. Unfortunately, acting out a story from the reading book or coloring a picture about a history lesson is not teaching to multiple intelligences. Just because there is some sound theory behind the notion that we construct our own learning does not mean that students naturally construct anything meaningful or educative when left on their own.

In Dewey's lifetime, as now, the first casualty of such "active learning" was subject matter, which always leaves professional educators easy targets to a variety of critics. Teachers during the early and middle years of the last century grabbed onto terms like "progressive education" and "the project method" and made them into empty, albeit at times fun, classroom actions. In the case of progressive education, what Dewey had articulated as a sophisticated and radical rethinking of existing education had, by the late 1940s, become associated with anything not related to the teaching of basic academic subjects. All bad teaching had become known as progressive education; and with some high schools providing classes in hypnotism and contract bridge in the name of progressive education, the critics might not have been far off (Cremin 1961; Martin 1951; Trillingham 1951).

What Did Dewey Mean?

None of this, however, does much to say what Dewey *did* mean by active learning. While the nature of this introduction does not allow for a careful treatment of this very important idea, there are four things you might keep in mind as you read the essays in this section.

First, Dewey never intended to set activity and subject matter against one another. Learning subject matter and learning through meaningful activity were not to be mutually exclusive. In fact, in *Experience and Education*, Dewey (1988, 10) argued strongly against an either/or mentality toward traditional and progressive education and reframed the problem of subject matter as one in which we have to decide how to help the "young become acquainted with the past in such a way that the acquaintance is a potent agent in appreciation of the living present." Moreover, even subject matter was to be seen as something active, as something "fluent, embryonic, vital" (Dewey 1976b, 278). To that end, Dewey (1988, 56) emphasized that while "the organized subject matter of the adult and the specialist cannot provide the starting point . . . it represents the goal toward which education should continuously move." Subject matter is a means and not an end in active learning.

Second, active learning is concerned with more than subject matter; active learning also implies social engagement. Dewey believed that traditional schooling in his time had failed to prepare young people for their roles in society because it had "erected silence into one of its prime virtues" (Dewey 1988, 40) and had endeavored "to prepare future members of the social order in a medium in which the conditions of the social spirit" were "eminently wanting" (Dewey 1976b, 10). Those schools had wasted an educational opportunity by failing to allow students to utilize the experiences they got outside the school in any "complete and free way within the school itself"; students were unable to "apply in daily life" what they learned in school (Dewey 1976a, 46). Active learning is most effective when it takes place in the context of an "embryonic community life, active with types of occupations that reflect the life of the larger society *and* [emphasis added] permeated throughout with the spirit of art, history, science" (Dewey 1976a, 19). Within these embryonic communities, active learning would saturate the students in a spirit of service and provide them with the instruments of self-direction.

Third, while Dewey encouraged a Copernican-like shift that would move the child to the center of the educational universe, active learning was not to be based on the child's impulsive and haphazard preferences. Instead, Dewey (1976a, 25) suggested that valuable educational results come most likely "through direction, through organized use." The teacher has the responsibility to channel the students' naturally intense activity by directing their activities, "giving them exercise along certain lines" (Dewey 1976a, 25). The teacher should indeed let students express their initial impulse; but then, the teacher's task is, "through criticism, question, and suggestion," to bring each student "to consciousness of what he has done and what he needs to do" (Dewey 1976a, 28). In sum, active learning that is also educative and meaningful happens when the teacher helps the child "to realize his own impulse by recognizing the facts, materials, and conditions involved, and then to regulate his impulse through that recognition" (Dewey 1976a, 27).

Finally, learning that is active takes place when viewed in the context of a continuum of individual intellectual development. Active learning that is educative, and not mis-educative, is characterized by continuity and growth. Continuity in education means that any learning experience that is organized for the student should take into consideration the experience the child brings to the learning activity and should prepare the child for future experiences. This criteria is *not* met, however, simply by helping students acquire skills they will need six years from now in college. Rather, preparation for the future means helping the student get out of the present experience "all that there is in it for him at the time in which he has it" (Dewey 1988, 29). More specifically (Dewey 1988, 29):

> *We always live at the time we live and not at some other time, and only by extracting at each present time the full meaning of each present experience are we prepared for doing the same thing in the future. This is the only preparation which in the long run amounts to anything.*

Reconsidering Hands-On Lessons

Another characteristic of meaningful active learning is *growth*. In *Experience and Education*, Dewey (1988) discussed growth as one aspect of continuity. I have chosen to treat it separately here for the sake of emphasizing its importance and our tendency to overlook its implications. Dewey warned that it is not sufficient to talk simply of growth as the result of activity. We must, instead, "specify the direction in which growth takes place" (Dewey 1988, 19):

> [F]rom the standpoint of growth as education and education as growth the question is whether growth in this direction promotes or retards growth in general. Does this form of growth create conditions for further growth, or does it set up conditions that shut off the person who has grown in this particular direction from the occasions, stimuli, and opportunities for continuing growth in new directions?

If teachers take this caution seriously, they will have to reconsider those "hands-on" activities in which they believe that students are constructing their own understandings. For it is possible that the understandings they construct could be undisciplined and even inaccurate. Moreover, because these activities are conducted with the teacher's approval, these understandings are assumed to be correct by the student, thus creating a false sense of certainty that might discourage future experimentation or openness and create barriers to new exploration.

Deweyan activity implies so much more than simple hands-on lessons and student movement around the room. Though active learning might be manifest in external movement, real active learning is cognitive and social. It is a process; it is communal; it is a growth experience; and it is continuous. Most of all, it requires a rethinking of your role as a teacher and learner in the classroom. As you read the following selections, read them with the characteristics of active learning in mind. Think in terms of how their content relates to your own experiences. Share them with your colleagues and challenge one another to examine your own practice in relation to what they have to say. Read them in the context of where you want to go as a teacher and how they might help you get there. Read them for all you can get out of them both for the teacher you are today and the teacher you hope to be tomorrow.

References

Cremin, L. 1961. *The transformation of the school: Progressivism in American education, 1876–1957*. New York: Vintage Books.

Dewey, J. 1976a. *The school and society*. In *John Dewey: The middle works, 1899–1924*, ed. J. A. Boydston, Vol. 1: 1899–1901, 1–112. Carbondale, IL: Southern Illinois University Press.

Dewey, J. 1976b. *The child and the curriculum*. In *John Dewey: The middle works, 1899–1924*, ed. J. A. Boydston, Vol. 2: 1902–1903, 271–92. Carbondale, IL: Southern Illinois University Press.

Dewey, J. 1980. *Democracy and education*. In *John Dewey: The middle works, 1899–1924*, ed. J. A. Boydston, Vol. 9: 1916, 1–402. Carbondale, IL: Southern Illinois University Press.

Dewey, J. 1988. *Experience and education*. In *John Dewey: The later works, 1925–1953*, ed. J. A. Boydston, Vol. 13: 1938–1939, 1–62. Carbondale, IL: Southern Illinois University Press.

Martin, L. 1951. Denver, Colorado. *Saturday Review of Literature*, Sept. 8: 6–13.

Trillingham, C. C. 1951. What's right with public education? *The School Executive* 70(40): 39–42.

— ∽ —

One
Active Learning as Reflective Experience

William H. Schubert

> *Mere activity does not constitute experience.*
> —*Democracy and Education*, MW 9: 146

When someone calls my office and reaches my answering machine, they hear some variation on: "You have reached the Schubertian Center for Curricular Speculation where we ponder what is worth knowing and experiencing. Please leave a message after the beep and have a good day and life." Note: The Schubertian Center is fictional and unfunded, which gives it great latitude in speculation that ranges from the subatomic to the everyday to the cosmic, and does not diminish its realness in a postmodern and Deweyan pragmatic sense.

While this message is partially offered with tongue-in-cheek humor, it also embodies a deep seriousness with which I have pursued education since my years as an elementary school teacher in the late 1960s and early 1970s. Today, too, the message remains central to doctoral students of curriculum studies, practicing teachers and school administrators who engage with me through courses or consultancies, and colleagues in the curriculum field.

Though my experience as an elementary school teacher occurred more than 30 years ago, I remember it vividly, and it still informs my endeavors as a professor today. Working with elementary students is always *active*, but it is not *experience* in the Deweyan sense if the activity does not embody reflection. Dewey (1980, 146) said that mere activity is "dispersive, centrifugal, dissipating." But serious reflection on activity can transform activity into growth experience.

My List of Activities

When I completed my elementary school teaching episode of life, knowing that my next episode was one of teaching teachers, I sat down to make a list of what I learned. I brainstormed about 150 activities that I considered successful; most of them started with student interests and concerns (Dewey's *psychological*) and led them to integrate funds of knowledge from experienced persons or disciplines of knowledge (Dewey's *logical*) with their own project of growing their life in a sociocultural context. Nevertheless, the list was one of mere activities—e.g., invent a language, create a game to teach younger children, make a family genealogy, use catalogs to find $1,000 worth of gifts to help someone in need, observe planet Earth as if you were extraterrestrial explorers, bring in broken things to repair, interview others about important matters, and on and on.

I remembered that these teaching strategies did not usually derive from completion of lesson plan forms or from writing behavioral objectives. Instead, they emerged as I experienced literature, art, and philosophy. I created spaces for myself to do this. Sometimes I found friends or colleagues who could ponder with me. This pondering stimulated my imagination and challenged the assumptions on which I based my life.

This calling to self-educate was my professional development. From the context it provided, I could invent possibilities with children—activities that started from a sense of direction and evolved through places that surprised us, stimulating wonder which lies at the heart of reflection. Reflection spurred by wonder, then, is a seed that transforms mere activity into experience. An "experience," as Dewey (1987) pointed out in *Art as Experience*, is making meaning of any dimension of one's life so that it connects who we are and have been with who we are striving to become.

Sources of Inspiration

As I pondered my list, I thought of the wonder inspired by art, literature, and philosophy that stimulated development of these activities. Then a shadow crept over my pondering as I thought of teacher in-service days. Usually, these days were one of two extremes: make-it-take-it or theory-research-sprinkled-with-jokes. The former showed how to make a specific project or lesson to use in the classroom. I recall a colorful, painted sun on burlap. All the suns looked about the same when displayed throughout the classroom. However, the project had no generativity. It was an activity only. The other extreme was the theorist or researcher who had a gig splotched with humor, after which teachers chuckled a bit while finding no direct relevance to their classroom.

I recall a case in which I thought such a research-oriented in-service was just plain wrong. The researcher said that students in the intermediate grades could not understand metaphorical thinking. He said that it was fruitless to try it with them. The researcher illustrated his point with the adage, "A rolling stone gathers no moss." He said that students would, at best, give a literal interpretation of such a statement. However, I had engaged in discussions with students that told me otherwise. So I followed with a study of my own. I returned to my sixth-grade students who were busy working on individualized projects and called them one-by-one to my desk, quietly whispering the illustrative adage to each and asking for an interpretation. Some could not relate; others gave literal interpretations of a stone on a mossy hill; a couple related it to The Rolling Stones; and several provided philosophic advice about the value of stopping to enjoy life. One immediately retorted with an adage of his own, which is still etched in my memory: "Well I guess it means that if you are a nail and don't get into hot water, then you won't get rusty." *This* was clearly more than mere activity!

Invention Strategies

So, as I pondered my list of 150 activities, I decided that I wanted to do teacher education that would speak to teachers' needs more fully than the make-it-take-it or dissemination of theory-research orientations. I wondered what enabled me to think of these activities. Was it the literature, art, and philosophy directly, or was there a more intermediate source of imagination? I expressed what I searched for—this intermediate point between make-it-take-it and research-theory—as *invention strategies*. Invention strategies, as I now consider them, were partially unconscious themes from the literature, art, and philosophy that helped me tailor activities from sources of meaning, concern, and interest in students' lives. I made a list of 20-some invention strategies, and for 30 years I have offered them to teachers who sought to enliven their teaching. Among these were limiting, traveling, playing, classifying, rating, interviewing, acting, doing, dialoging, conversing, playing, dreaming, daydreaming, producing, gaming, and feeling (carried away with gerands). If a teacher can't think of an interesting lesson, I encourage focus on one of the invention strategies. For example, with *traveling*: travel back to a specific time period or to a literary scene and act out how it might feel to be there; or travel in a molecule through the circulatory system; or plan a trip through the continent of Africa (noting language phrases, monetary units, historical places to see, cultural ways, places to stay, customs, climate, sites to see, foods, and traditions). With *playing*, try to reinvigorate the desire to play—noting that when students enter school, pompous adults tell them that play (their mode of learning that taught them more in the first five years of life than they will learn in the rest) is over, and work (too often drudgery) has begun. Play, like travel, can transform education from activity to experience, because inherent in it is a continuous recreating of oneself in a sociocultural context. Space, here, does not permit elaboration on all of the invention strategies. (I am contemplating a book to do this.)

The point behind invention strategies is that these strategies are processes born of reflection on central sources of wonder in human life. Robert Ulich (1955, 255) characterized them vividly as "the great mysteries and events of life: birth, death, love, tradition, society and the crowd, success and failure, salvation, and anxiety." If activities embody such concerns, and invention strategies often do, they constitute experience. They integrate remembrance of one's past and anticipation of one's future in the search for present meaning.

What to Reflect On

For 15 years since I developed the invention strategies, I admonished teachers and school leaders to reflect. Then a well-known educational scholar who visited our university conducted a colloquium in which he raised an issue that astounded me, because I thought everyone already knew the answer. He said something to this effect: "Everyone tells teachers to reflect, but no one says what it is that they should reflect on." Then, I thought that perhaps I had too little empathy for teachers who work amid a swirl of activity, without enough time to reflectively experience it. So I made another list, which I have used as a basis for discussion in classes and workshops. I share them here, knowing full well that it would be better if space permitted elaboration. (I think I might include this in the book, too, or create yet another book.)

1. Reflect on education as a calling that enables personal and social growth.
2. Reflect on what you have to share (your strengths).
3. Reflect on what is worth knowing and experiencing.
4. Reflect on who decides (and should decide) this.
5. Reflect on who benefits (and who does not) from such decisions.
6. Reflect on yourself as a curriculum for others.
7. Reflect on others as a curriculum for you.
8. Reflect on the most important things you have learned (e.g., knowledge, skills, values, appreciations, interests, dispositions).
9. Reflect on how, where, and under what circumstance you learned them.
10. Reflect on the hidden curriculum of your educational setting, i.e., what is taught and learned by the context, rules, and expectations.
11. Reflect on what is learned by the out-of-school experiences (outside curriculum) of your students (e.g., from homes, families, mass media, work, hobbies, non-school organizations, peer relationships).
12. Reflect on how to identify and build on students' strengths.
13. Reflect on what it means to broaden and deepen students' perspectives and abilities.
14. Reflect on how to speak the multiple languages of students.
15. Reflect on how to feel the hurt and joy inside students.

16. Reflect on the balance between realities and ideals in education.
17. Reflect on the central, driving ideas that you embody, i.e., that are part of who you are as a person . . . as a teacher.
18. Reflect on what you want to contribute to others as an educator through knowledge, skills, values, social reform, personal growth, and spiritual connectedness.
19. Reflect on what you have learned each day.
20. Reflect on why reflection helps and what else to reflect on.

This last call for reflection epitomizes the essence of Dewey's distinction between activity and experience. To engage in Deweyan experience requires continuous revisiting of such reflections, never considering them fully answered, and making them one with the process of living. So, this is what I mean by my encouragement to ponder in my message on the telephone answering machine at the Schubertian Center!

References

Dewey, J. 1980. *Democracy and education.* In *John Dewey: The middle works, 1899–1924*, ed. J. A. Boydston, Vol. 9: 1916, 1–402. Carbondale, IL: Southern Illinois University Press.

Dewey, J. 1987. *Art as experience.* In *John Dewey: The later works, 1925–1953*, ed. J. A. Boydston, Vol. 10: 1934, 1–456. Carbondale, IL: Southern Illinois University Press.

Ulich, R. 1955. Comments on Ralph Harper's essay. In *Modern philosophies of education*, The fifty-fourth yearbook of the National Society for the Study of Education, Part I, ed. N. B. Henry, 254–57. Chicago: University of Chicago Press.

— ∽ —

Two

'Impulsive Expression': Desirable or Dangerous?

Robert H. Anderson

> *The child is already intensely active, and the question of education is the question of taking hold of his activities, of giving them direction. Through direction, through organized use, they tend toward valuable results, instead of scattering or being left to merely impulsive expression.*
> —*The School and Society*, MW 1: 25

Dewey's work is almost literally timeless, and therefore a long-ago quote such as the one on which this essay is based could be readily recognized as remaining applicable to children and their educational needs in this early part of the 21st century. This is true even though rather dramatic changes have taken place in family life and in the needs and interests of children over recent years. These changes have had almost mind-boggling implications for the growth and development of children, and therefore for the nature of the educational environment that must exist if children are to thrive within it. Yet one could imagine that Dewey had at least premonitions of these very conditions in his mind in that long-ago era.

Considering Today's Complications

While Dewey in this century might choose to use a somewhat different phrase from "taking hold of [the child's] activities" when identifying a key question on which to concentrate, it seems that giving students direction remains a useful definition of at least a major dimension of teachers' work. In at least one respect, symbolized by the increasing significance of child-controlled computers, functions of direction and of the organized use of results have become somewhat clearer than they were throughout most of the prior century. Yet, at the same time, there are more complications with which to deal: a far greater percentage of students identified as having "special needs"; much stronger pressure from the testing industry and its advocates toward conformity; increasing numbers of teachers (especially in schools serving the "underclass") with serious deficits in preparation; and what can be reasonably described as critically insufficient financial support for schooling within most of society.

Achieving 'Valuable Results'

When Dewey identified what he called "scattering or being left to merely impulsive expression" as undesirable, he was doubtlessly commenting critically upon a certain looseness that may have prevailed at the time in many schools. However, from his many writings, it was clear that Dewey had great respect for the innate intelligence of children and also for the desirability of skillful and sympathetic direction of each child's activities. One can transpose such views into a perception on Dewey's part of children as highly educable, positively motivated, and capable of achieving "valuable results."

Debating 'Impulsive Expression'

It would be instructive, and probably exciting as well, to create a scenario to be enacted at this point in the 21st century, within which might be debated a phrase such as "impulsive expression." Conceivably, Dewey could write a script to guide both of the arguments relative to that phrase as reflecting either a desideratum, on the one hand, or a situation or danger to be avoided, on the other. From the context of Dewey's paragraph, it would seem that he would choose to defend the "danger" argument. From some of his other writings, however, it could well be that any commitment on his part to the alternative of danger would be somewhat muted.

Already implied here was that Dewey had great respect for children, at least insofar as the potential for highly productive activity is concerned. It also is clear that he had high hopes for the significant improvement of human life through appropriate and skillfully orchestrated educational processes. That his ideas and proposals for making schooling a more productive and well-coordinated enterprise have had such a salutary impact upon practice over so many decades is a tribute not only to him but also to the many educators who shared his viewpoint and, perhaps especially, his commitment to enabling the great potential of children to ripen and prosper. May the wisdom he shared through his work and writings be ever valued, and constantly accepted as worth sustaining.

Reference

Dewey, J. 1976. *The school and society*. In *John Dewey: The middle works, 1899–1924*, ed. J. A. Boydston, Vol. 1: 1899–1901, 1–112. Carbondale, IL: Southern Illinois University Press.

— ∽ —

Three

Work in School

Donna Adair Breault

> *There is very little place in the traditional schoolroom for the child to work.*
> —The School and Society, MW 1: 22

As an assistant principal, I had the pleasure of bus duty each day. This was one of my favorite administrative tasks because it enabled me to watch the children as they began and ended their days at school. One thing I always noticed was the amazing amount of energy the students had at the end of the day. I often had to help them "contain" that energy as they hurried to their buses. In contrast, I would enter the school building at the end of bus duty and see some of the teachers dragging themselves to their mailboxes, utterly exhausted. It was quite clear from my observations that these teachers had done all the work, not their students. This fact was supported by my visits to these teachers' rooms where I would see them spend hours pulling together information to give to their students and then additional hours reading the worksheets the students completed to demonstrate that they had received the information.

Who Is Doing the Work?

I believe Dewey (1976) addressed the situation best in *School and Society*, when he described the trouble he had finding desks for his laboratory school. He noted that after looking in shop after shop, one salesperson finally commented that he wanted tables where children could work, but the shop only had desks where children could listen. Similarly, in *Democracy and Education* (1980, 44), he lamented,

> *Why is it, in spite of the fact that teaching by pouring in, learning by passive absorption, are universally condemned, that they are still so entrenched in practice? That teaching is not an affair of 'telling' and being told, but an active and constructive process is a principle almost as generally violated in practice as conceded in theory.*

Wong and Wong (1991) concur. In their book *The First Days of School*, they reminded their audience of new and practicing teachers that the person who is doing the work in the classroom is the person who is learning.

Why do teachers seem to have the tendency to do all the work in their classrooms? I can speak only from personal experience. When I first started teaching, I felt such a tremendous responsibility for the academic and emotional well-being of my second graders. While I did not fall into the workbook and worksheet routine, I nevertheless recall spending countless hours making manipulatives and creating learning centers all evolving around weekly themes: outer space, the sea, insects, etc.

Meanwhile, I was coming to my class intellectually unprepared. I knew very little about the subjects I "taught"—dinosaurs, planets, plants, and animals. I had plenty of cute activities, but I did not have the grounding through which I could ask the truly meaningful questions. Without that grounding, I was forced into the role of entertainer instead of being a facilitator for higher levels of learning. As such, I created a vicious cycle for myself. Staying busy with the cute activities and manipulatives prevented me from spending time learning and modeling learning. Without the deeper knowledge of the subject matter, I had little choice but to continue entertaining.

Intellectually Engaging Activities

Over time I learned from my many mistakes. I realized *entertaining* activities and *intellectually engaging* activities were not synonymous. I began to reassess my priorities and use of time to make sure the experiences I provided for my students were first and foremost educative—whether or not they resulted in something that would make a great display outside my classroom door. Most importantly, I realized the critical prerequisites for the kind of active learning Dewey described throughout his work: thoughtful planning, solid understanding of the subject matter, a willingness to experience ambiguity in the learning context, and a relationship of mutual trust between the teacher and the students. Seems like a tall order, doesn't it?

I recall a beautiful example of this type of active learning from a first-year teacher I once observed. This teacher was using a math word problem as the focus of her lesson that day. The fifth-grade students were given a piece of paper with an outline of a shopping mall and stores of various shapes and sizes. The only information provided for the students was the monthly rent for one of the stores. No store dimensions were provided. They had to determine an appropriate monthly rent for all the other stores in the mall diagram.

The students, already divided into teams, immediately began working on the problem. They knew where the necessary materials—the rulers, calculators, etc.— were located in the room, and they knew they could use them when needed as long as they returned them to their appropriate places. The teacher walked around the room, commenting about each group's progress, posing challenging questions, and responding to students' questions with additional questions to deepen the level of thinking on the project. There was no need for the teacher to remind students to stay on task or to provide any sort of extrinsic motivation for good behavior. They were very interested in the problem, and they hardly noticed others around them as they worked. Like many elementary classrooms, this lesson was interrupted by their lunchtime and their physical education period; but after each interruption the students eagerly picked up where they had left off.

Many of the groups of students took very different routes to solving their math problem. They used multiple forms of computation, including multiplication and division and working with fractions. Some groups recalled formulas to determine the area of spaces, while others found common units of measurement from various objects in the room. The teacher, well-grounded in math, was able to facilitate each of the different routes the groups took. Ultimately, students provided thoughtful suggestions for rent along with justifications for those prices. In addition, each group assessed its effectiveness in problem solving based on a critical thinking rubric provided by the teacher.

What made this lesson an exemplar of active learning in a Deweyan sense? The students were intellectually engaged with a meaningful purpose. They were able to use their experiences and their collective understanding of math to solve a problem. Further, they were able to see themselves as problem solvers and recognize the significance of their capacity to think. This first-year teacher had achieved something it took me years to achieve. She had created a dynamic classroom environment where active learning through meaningful engagement—not activity generated through entertainment—was the force and focus of her instruction.

References

Dewey, J. 1976. *The school and society*. In *John Dewey: The middle works, 1899–1924*, ed. J. A. Boydston, Vol. 1: 1899–1901, 1–112. Carbondale, IL: Southern Illinois University Press.

Dewey, J. 1980. *Democracy and education*. In *John Dewey: The middle works, 1899–1924*, ed. J. A. Boydston, Vol. 9: 1916, 1–402. Carbondale, IL: Southern Illinois University Press.

Wong, H. K., and R. T. Wong. 1991. *The first days of school*. Sunnyvale, CA: Harry K. Wong Publications.

— ∽ —

Four
Becoming a Student of Teaching
Robert V. Bullough, Jr.

> The teacher who leaves the professional schools with power in managing a class of children may appear to superior advantage the first day, the first week, the first month, or even the first year, as compared with some other teacher who has a much more vital command of psychology, logic, and ethics of development. But later 'progress' may with such consist only in perfecting and refining skill already possessed. Such persons seem to know how to teach, but they are not students of teaching. . . . Unless a teacher is such a student, he may continue to improve in the mechanics of school management, but he can not grow as a teacher.
> —The Relation of Theory to Practice in Education, MW 3: 256

When educators speak about their teacher preparation, they commonly use the word "training" to describe the process. We tell others that we attended a teacher-training program at a university or college. We graduated trained and certified to teach. It is easy to dismiss use of this term by saying, "Oh, it's just a word." But words name worlds and form realities; and the use of this particular word brings with it much mischief, as Dewey implied.

Dogs are trained by their masters to walk on their hind legs and beg for a biscuit. Elephants are trained to sit on a barrel, raise their trunks to the sky, and trumpet for adoring crowds. On the human side, soldiers, among others, also are trained. On the darkest of nights, infantry soldiers can disassemble and reassemble M-16 rifles with staggering speed. Soldiers are trained to react, and react swiftly and seemingly without thought to signs of danger. Through drill and practice, responses are wired in. When facing danger, procedures that have been learned click in and direct action. In each of these examples, four-legged and two-legged, ends are known in advance. There is no room for deviation nor for individual initiative. So it is in teaching, as Dewey suggested, that an emphasis on training over education leaves little room for teacher growth.

Recognizing Potential in the Unexpected

In teaching, outcomes are rarely, if ever, predictable. No matter how hard we try to manage teaching and to make our actions produce the results intended by us or desired by others, they never do—not quite. When teaching, something inevitably happens that disrupts the flow of the day and forces the setting aside of even the most carefully crafted plan. Something more important for learning suddenly presents itself to us, or something grimly insistent comes along and demands precious classroom time and moral space: A child gets hurt and tears flow; a dirty joke is told, a gasp heard, and muffled and disruptive conversation ensues; a child realizes an amazing and unexpected achievement, and spontaneously the class erupts into clapping and loud cheering; Snowball, the beloved class rabbit, gets sick and dies; and, looking outside the school walls, a space shuttle explodes or two airplanes slam into the World Trade Center.

To manage uncertainty, teachers need procedural knowledge, knowledge of routines, and the ability to implement them. But given the nature of our work and of the work context, teaching routines often stretch and snap, and our teacher habits fail. Then what? At that moment, teachers face a choice: Exercising power, they can bring punishments and rewards to bear in the attempt to reestablish a failed routine by altering the context to better fit that routine; they can switch to another routine (assuming another is known); or they can reconsider the entire situation and reorganize it to achieve another and different end. The last response is only possible when the teacher understands self, teaching, and the context of teaching deeply and richly; when the teacher is educated, not merely trained, to teach and is a student of teaching, just as Dewey suggested. Otherwise, routines define the day and, in defining the day, bind the teacher and limit learning. Maintaining routines becomes the end of education rather than a means for its achievement.

Realizing Personal Potential

Dewey's statement requires consideration here of an additional word and distinction: the word is "professional." Over the past few decades, designating someone a professional has lost much of its meaning and nearly all of its cachet. It is a word that has been co-opted by barbers, plumbers, and, if we can believe the movies, hired killers. But the distinctive feature and defining characteristic of a professional compared to a nonprofessional is that the professional learns from experience: The professional is a student of his or her own practice and development and, in studying that practice and development, is one who constantly grows in understanding and in ability.

In the hands of professionals, a practice becomes increasingly personal, nuanced, and subtle; and problems—when something does not unfold as anticipated or falls outside of preferred practice—are taken as invitations to reconsider personal and professional beliefs, knowledge, including of subject matter, and skills and not as reasons for dismay or disillusionment. Problems are invitations to get deeper into ourselves, those we teach, our subject matter, and our situations. Ever-learning, the professional teacher knows himself or herself well, and seeks to uncover blind spots, prejudices, and weaknesses, as well as to discover strengths upon which to build. He or she is forward looking, imagining then seeking better and more interesting ways of being with and for young people. Self-critical, the professional can attribute causes, but does so in humility and without placing blame. Instead, he or she accepts responsibility for his or her actions and their educational consequences.

Like trained teachers, newcomers to teaching often look outside of themselves when something goes awry. They tend to blame others, their own teachers, cooperating teachers, and their teacher-education programs, as well as their students and their backgrounds, for failure. Having long been the recipients of teacher classroom offerings, they tend to assume that teaching is a simple matter: one dispenses what one knows and disciplines recalcitrants. Not being privy to the professional's inner logic, its evolution, nor to the origins of that logic, they inevitably underappreciate the difficulty and complexity of effective teaching. Assuming that one learns to teach by teaching—one just does it—they sometimes succumb to the temptation to reduce especially artful performance to a matter of time and training, of learning, and then practicing the application of a few rules that folk wisdom and occasionally researchers promise will lead to skilled practice. But, the promise inevitably proves to be only somewhat or sometimes true. This is one of the sources of what, among beginners, is called "reality shock"— the discovery that teaching is not quite as easy as it looked from the student side of the teacher's desk and that learning to teach is much more difficult than ever imagined. Practice, they discover, does not make perfect, especially when practice is made routine and inflexible. Nor does mimicry equal mastery.

Making Opportunities out of Chaos

Teachers are surrounded by events that call forth wonder and surprise, and it is precisely these emotions that make teaching potentially such an interesting and satisfying relationship and a fascinating and fulfilling form of human expression. Only teachers who are students of teaching, who are knowledgeable and engaged professionals, who are morally centered, and who can flexibly and purposefully respond to the shifting emotional and intellectual terrain of the classroom, are capable of realizing this potential or even of recognizing it. Students of teaching know that chaos is forever residing just around the corner and that teachers face it mostly alone. They feel vulnerable and exposed, but not fearful; for they also know that opportunity stands just around that corner, and they are prepared and willing to embrace it. If, as teachers, we are merely trained and are generally fearful of failure and desirous to contain the unexpected, we are going to miss the opportunities for growth that teaching provides—perhaps not today, but most assuredly tomorrow. Clearly, teaching is not for the feint of heart, but a calling for the adventurous of mind and spirit.

Reference

Dewey, J. 1977. The relation of theory to practice in education. In *John Dewey: The middle works, 1899–1924*, ed. J. A. Boydston, Vol. 3: 1903–1906, 249–72. Carbondale, IL: Southern Illinois University Press.

— ✧ —

Five

Disdain for the 'Pouring in' Process

Frank E. Marsh

> *Why is it, in spite of the fact that teaching by pouring in, learning by passive absorption, are universally condemned, that they are still so entrenched in practice? That education is not an affair of 'telling' and being told, but an active and constructive process is a principle almost as generally violated in practice as conceded in theory.*
> —*Democracy and Education*, MW 9: 43

These words, penned nearly 60 years ago, strike at the central theme of the Dewey thesis. They reflect his disdain for the current practice as he viewed it, as well as its underlying psychological principles and philosophy. Dewey found the approaches of European writers and scholars inadequate to provide a solid foundation for a psychology and philosophy to be applied to an individual child. They were too stylized and inflexible and failed to address the individual differences that he observed in children. He determined that a totally new and different approach was needed. The ever-changing aspects of human experience made imperative a more empirical approach. He adopted what has come to be called "pragmatism." Many people accept this as the original American philosophy.

Dewey has been described as the first educational thinker to provide for the teacher-essential elements for a successful learning experience. He presented a philosophical framework for an educational enterprise that viewed schools as an integrated part of a free society, vital to a successful democracy. He followed this with a rational psychology of learning that emphasized the active nature of the learning process. His philosophy implied methodology for viewing knowledge, which included ways of selecting objectives and structuring lessons to facilitate the active process of learning.

Individualized Learning

Though students are grouped for learning, a teacher must realize that learning is a highly individualized process. The "pouring in" process is totally unsatisfactory. Many teachers conceive of learning in terms of the material to be covered rather than in terms of the varied and irregular experiences that individual students bring to the classroom. One only has to visit classrooms, view the lesson plans of many teachers, or study the curriculum guides of various states or school districts to see that the "pouring in" approach described by Dewey is still widely used. Inherent in the current emphasis upon mandated regular testing is the conclusion that "pouring in" is still very much in vogue.

Pragmatism, as espoused by Dewey, maintains that there is no hierarchy of studies and that the goals of learning emerge from the past experience, needs, and interests of the individual learner. To implement these goals in a classroom is a complex and challenging enterprise. Dewey called on teachers to move away from the highly specific and quantified goals and the classically oriented curricula of the past. Realistically, most teachers are not prepared to approach teaching in this way, and a vast reeducation effort would be needed to bring about change.

Dewey's classroom would be far more student-oriented and less teacher-centered than is the current mode. Because students bring highly varied experiences, interests, and skills to the classroom, activities must be varied to assist individual learners to engage in the learning process in meaningful ways.

The role of the teacher must likewise change. In place of "pouring in," the teacher must discover where each learner is, help establish relevant goals, and assist in moving each learner toward a desired goal. The typical classroom would have students engaged in various activities rather than quietly sitting listening or joining with fellow students in common experiences.

Evaluation of learning must not assume that a common base of factual knowledge, understandings, or skills exists that can be measured and assigned a numerical or letter grade. New concepts of measuring and grading must be established. Grading should reflect the degree to which each learner has moved toward established goals rather than the result of an application of a predetermined quantitative standard.

Today's Influences on Educational Practice

Before attempting to evaluate the profound effects of Dewey's work and theories upon modern practice, attention must be called to several factors that should and have influenced educational practice. The teaching profession has made spectacular advances. From the one-room schoolhouse, teaching has moved to modern educational centers. States have established departments of education that set standards for both teachers and curriculum. Financial support, however inadequate, provides and requires basic standards.

Preparation of teachers has been strengthened. Certification of programs as well as of individual teachers guarantees that all teachers have earned credentials. The advent of teachers associations and unions has tried to give educators a unified voice and influence over not only how they teach but what they teach, as well as over working conditions. An ancillary result of this movement is that the educational process has become politicized. Teachers are no longer considered a powerless group of low-paid public servants. They are now viewed as a vocal political force, well-organized, and competing for tax dollars.

Technology has had a profound effect upon educational practice. Television is but one of the communication marvels that vastly expands the learning and teaching resources now available in every classroom. School consolidation has brought about better-equipped and staffed facilities. Perhaps the most profound of these resources is the personal computer. Schools are rapidly making computer literacy an integral tool. Today's primary age students have an amazing ability to master these skills and understandings.

Vocational and technical education has been added and strengthened to provide richer and more practical offerings for young people. Most of these programs build upon basic knowledge and citizenship training to teach skills that enhance immediate employment for graduates. Industrial society demands these programs.

These and other factors have influenced educational practice. Before briefly examining the implications of Dewey's theories upon today's practice, certain generalizations must be made. Still today, most learning takes place in a group setting. Many of the changes and advances discussed earlier could greatly enhance the individualization of teaching. The personal computer, perhaps more than anything, opens vast possibilities for individualized learning in a variety of settings. To be fair, we must acknowledge that progress has lagged. There is a reluctance to embrace change.

Rediscovering Fundamental Truths

It can be argued that John Dewey lived and worked in and for another age. This, however, is indeed a shortsighted view. The basic underpinning of his writings is sound and is still crying out for recognition and application. Notably, education is fundamental to a free society. Moreover, learning is the reorganization of experience and is hence a highly individualized endeavor. Any attempt to force (pour in) learning en masse is doomed to failure for both individuals and society.

Adequate time has passed for us to evaluate Dewey's influence on educational theory and practice. We must note that our world is vastly different from the world in which Dewey lived and worked. Despite these differences, Dewey's influences are clearly visible. Throughout the years, as well as today, educators have sought ways to implement Dewey's wisdom into practice. Good teachers seek ways to individualize instruction, to provide for individual differences for a student population with widely different needs, interests, and potentialities. We are ever conscious of the challenges brought to us by learners with special needs. They are no longer ignored and neglected, but are being integrated into our classes.

Rather than allocating Dewey's work to the dustpan of history or viewing him as a relic of the past, we should conclude that the fundamentals of his teachings are far more applicable in today's cyber-society than they were when originally conceived. To rediscover these fundamental truths and find ways to apply them offers us an exciting and challenging task.

Reference

Dewey, J. 1980. *Democracy and education*. In *John Dewey: The middle works, 1899–1924*, ed. J. A. Boydston, Vol. 9: 1916, 1–402. Carbondale, IL: Southern Illinois University Press.

— ∽ —

Six
Listening for the Gentle Whisper

Rick Breault

> *Will the proposed activity give that sort of expression to these impulses that will carry the child on to a higher plane of consciousness and action, instead of merely exciting him and then leaving him just where he was before, plus a certain amount of nervous exhaustion and appetite for more excitement in the future?*
> —The School and Society, MW 1: 84

The prophet Elijah stood at the entrance to the cave where he was spending the night while fleeing his enemies. God had told him to wait there and he would soon experience the presence of the Lord. As he waited, he first experienced a powerful wind that "shattered rocks." Next came an earthquake, then a fire. Each time, Elijah expected the presence of God to be in overwhelming expressions of natural power. Each time, he was wrong. After the fire came "a gentle whisper," and it was in that whisper that the prophet heard the voice of God and was strengthened to return and confront his enemies (*1 Kings* 19: 8–13 in Scofield 1984). Elijah expected to be awed by the physical presence of God. He was waiting for the excitement. The excitement, however, left him where he had been before—unfulfilled and still waiting. Only when he learned to be still and listen for a gentle whisper did that enlightenment come.

This is one of the first stories that came to mind the first time I read the quotation from *The School and Society*. Much in a child's world comes across like a sensory jackhammer—fast, loud, and repetitive. Nearly 20 years ago, Neil Postman (1985) observed that the average length of a shot on network television was only 3.5 seconds. That was before the influence of MTV and the quick-cut, shaky, handheld video used in so many current television shows and advertisements. In the same book, Postman described the Lincoln-Douglas debates in which each candidate spoke for two to three hours and hardly lost an audience member. Compare that to modern political debates in which candidates have no more than a few minutes to make or rebut a statement and to summarize their positions.

Toward a 'Higher Plane of Consciousness'

With rare exceptions, the entertainment industry seems to tell us that everything we need to know about any given issue, product, or scene can and should be taken in several seconds. Any more than that is time that could be spent putting yet another issue, product, or scene in front of you. Besides, if you get too close a look, you just might see that nothing was worth looking at in the first place. There seems to be little chance that the child will be able to hear, or even to know to listen for, the gentle whisper that might carry him or her to what Dewey called a "higher plane of consciousness and action."

An article I read reported a problem that occurred during an Oscar telecast: the high-definition image was unforgiving of the various natural physical "flaws" such as an actress's less-than-perfect complexion or an actor's signs of old age. I believe that "high definition" is exactly the kind of curriculum that Dewey would like us to implement. This type of curriculum and teaching would lead to deeper and more insightful learning. It would be a curriculum that required students to listen for the gentle whisper of intellectual reflection and engage in the intense gaze of scientific inquiry. That sort of curriculum is unlikely to excite the student in the way he or she typically expects to be excited. And Dewey would have said that's a good thing.

The excitement children experience in their entertainment leaves them addicted only for more excitement or, more accurately, agitation or stimulation. Children used to that kind of excitement become adults who require a 30-second shot clock so they do not have to wait too long for another basket. They need computers that are ever faster and meals that are fast and easy to "fit their busy lifestyle." Dewey's words, therefore, present a challenge and a bit of a quandary for me in my role as a teacher and now as a teacher educator. Amid those rushing images, do we need to adjust today's curriculum and teaching to a new generation of children who were raised on video games and 100-plus cable channels?

A Conducive Learning Environment

Years before I first read the quotation I chose here, I taught fifth grade. On days when achievement tests were being given and the kids were under stress (though nothing compared to the stress kids feel now that none of them are being left behind), I would begin the morning with a brief session of progressive relaxation—a technique in which one focuses on certain muscle groups, tensing and relaxing them one group at a time. I remember being disturbed by how many students simply could not be still.

More recently, the parents of a fourth-grade boy shared with me what happened during a visit to a medical specialist to get advice regarding their son's nervous tics. The specialist told them not to worry too much because, "It's pretty common among kids nowadays because of all their activities and schoolwork." As appalling as was the physician's response, I found the cultural situation that led to his observation to be just as frightening. Is today's learning environment one that Dewey would have believed to be conducive to carrying a child "on to a higher plane of consciousness"?

References

Dewey, J. 1976. *The school and society.* In *John Dewey: The middle works, 1899–1924*, ed. J. A. Boydston, Vol. 1: 1899–1901, 1–112. Carbondale, IL: Southern Illinois University Press.

Postman, N. 1985. *Amusing ourselves to death: Public discourse in the age of show business.* New York: Penguin.

Scofield, C. I., ed. 1984. *Oxford NIV Scofield study Bible.* New York: Oxford University Press.

— ∞ —

Seven

Providing Environments Conducive to Proper Digestion

Lisa Goeken-Galliart

> *It is as if the child were forever tasting and never eating; always having his palate tickled upon the emotional side, but never getting the organic satisfaction that comes only with the digestion of food and the transformation of it into working power.*
> —*The Child and the Curriculum*, MW 2: 281

John Dewey's quotation from *The Child and the Curriculum* is just as timely today as it was more than 100 years ago . . . or is it even more so? With the frenzied way in which we travel through our two-inched textbooks, our curriculum guides, our lessons, and our days, it is difficult to imagine that Dewey would be impressed. He probably would be saddened and disappointed that adults have evolved into such hurried creatures, but he most likely would be devastated by the way we are modeling and pouring it into our children's lives as well.

Making Connections Takes Time

Our world is so compulsive, immediate, and reactive that we just seem to ramble on without much thought. Our children are doing the same thing as they mirror their parents' lives. Children are not making connections, and that is because that process takes *time*. We are so convinced that there is not enough time, and we are so scheduled, that we miss the newness, the inspiration, and the wonder of it all! That is precisely what Dewey was cognizant of in 1902 and what he meant by "forever tasting and never eating."

In the classroom, teachers have to make decisions about how best to spend every minute of the day; time is a precious commodity and it must be spent wisely. That is not at all an overexaggeration or oversimplification. Every minute matters, and each one needs to be viewed as a learning opportunity. How a teacher chooses to use those minutes is an individual decision that is based on experience, attitude, knowledge, and philosophy. Dewey taught us that a chance to "strike while the iron is hot" should not be neglected, but seen as a once-in-a-lifetime opportunity that realistically may not come again. He knew that it is the teacher who is ultimately responsible for providing the environmental conditions necessary to guide a thought or an action—a process that involves the senses, movement, and missteps taken during the journey, and many times a sense of not knowing.

A Taste Is Not Enough

When practitioners skim the surface of a unit or topic of study, Dewey would say that we are giving the child only a "taste." Per his quote, he argued that this is simply not enough. By going into depth, one can "digest." Further, the "transformation into working power" is the empowerment students gain from being able and prepared to apply what was learned previously to new situations.

When we allow students to struggle with a problem and include the extra "space" needed in the day to do so, we help to provide the type of learning environment and appropriate stimuli needed to aid digestion. When we fail to resist the urge to rush in and provide comfort, when we control a given situation too tightly, or when we tell an answer too quickly, we clog up the system. Practitioners need to trust in collaboration and risk taking so that students can see the benefits of their newfound discoveries. This process allows transformation to take place.

Learning is active; it is moving and flurried; and, many times, it is loud. Many classrooms and schools need to adapt to allow this "movement" versus the mindless, orderly, and passive style that Dewey called "pouring in." He knew that this was unacceptable back in the early 1900s, and he would not find it palatable to discover it still being practiced in some classrooms today.

Processing the Big Ideas

He would applaud those who take the big ideas and process through them so thoroughly and thoughtfully, enabling students to explore, make the best use of carefully selected stimuli, and draw inferences on new topics. By going "deep" and not "long," Dewey would say that teachers are emphasizing the process and realizing the interdependence of it to the outcome. Students are then better able to let ideas emulsify, to note relevance, to apply new principles to other experiences, to inquire about different situations, and to persevere through the whole process with a sense of true and earned accomplishment.

Dewey's thoughts on this topic are arguably even more relevant today because of the time schedules chosen and placed upon the inhabitants of this new century. As the curriculum continues to become more and more multitudinous, teachers will need to challenge themselves even more so to find "space" within their own classroom schedules for some real "digestion" and "transformation." This "freeing up" may be a 100-year-old notion, but if implemented promptly, may save a generation from a serious case of indigestion!

Reference

Dewey, J. 1976. *The child and the curriculum.* In *John Dewey: The middle works, 1899–1924,* ed. J. A. Boydston, Vol. 2: 1902–1903, 271–92. Carbondale, IL: Southern Illinois University Press.

— ∽ —

PART II
THE EDUCATIVE EXPERIENCE

An Educative Experience?
A Lesson in Humility
for a Second-Grade Teacher

Donna Adair Breault

What am I going to do today? The question in my head kept getting louder as I approached the school building that morning. It was the next to last day of school. All papers and books had gone out the door with students the previous day, along with the plans I originally made for our time. To find something to keep them occupied and me sane for the next two days was a looming challenge. As I paused at a stoplight, it hit me! I pulled into a convenience store, picked up a pile of real estate magazines, and continued on my way to school, somewhat relieved.

"Class, we are going to spend the next two days building a city," I announced to my second graders. We spent the first part of the morning discussing what constitutes a city—subdivisions, stores, schools, churches, etc.—and then divided into teams to plan how we would proceed. Well before lunch, all the desks were pushed out of the way, and green, white, and gray bulletin board paper was unfurled across the classroom floor.

I won't say that the two-day activity was carried out in perfect pedagogical form. There were mistakes—largely because of poor planning. Discussions about the location of major roads, noise pollution from retail areas and its effects on nearby houses, and challenges regarding traffic around business areas came a bit too late to change some of the designs already carved out in magic marker. In the end, the city plan would not have won any great awards, but the primary goals—keeping students occupied and the teacher sane—had been achieved. As students said their final goodbyes and left for the summer break, I felt relieved and frankly a bit cocky about the events that had unfolded over those final two days.

Culminating Experiences

Years later, as a teacher educator always in search of anecdotes, I would recall the experience as my students read Dewey's *The School and Society* (1976a) and *The Child and the Curriculum* (1976b), and we would discuss "educative experiences." I believed that the activity was educative because students were actively engaged in cooperative learning and the curriculum was integrated, to a degree. I even would go so far as to say that some learning was going on—as much as I would have expected at the time given that it was the last two days of school.

And then I saw it! I ran across a book written by Ida DePencier (1967)—a former teacher from Dewey's lab school. As I was browsing through the book, one picture in particular caught my eye. It was a group of young students, possibly kindergarten or first graders, busy on the floor of their classroom building a city. My first response was, "Look, they are doing the same activity my students did." It didn't take long for me to realize how wrong I was. The caption under the picture noted: "A primary class builds a city. In addition to ideas in social studies, reading and mathematics played a large part of this activity. Ideas about zoning and city growth patterns became obvious" (DePencier 1967, 151). The more I discovered about Dewey's lab school, the more I realized that activities in that setting did far more than merely keep students occupied. They were culminating experiences through which students actively applied what they had learned in meaningful ways.

With this realization, images of what I could have done those last two days besieged me. In what ways could we have reviewed elements of geometry—including area, and parallel and perpendicular lines—as we planned our subdivisions? Rather than just letting students have free reign to draw squiggly lines across the page to represent subdivision roads and paste homes wherever they would fit, we could have discussed electrical, water, and sewage line issues and deliberately planned the location of streets and placement of houses. Had I thought to introduce the idea of zoning, I would have offered students a tremendous opportunity to debate the percentage of area within the city they would allot for commercial development. They would have been able to consider the issues surrounding the location of business areas, the number of businesses to allow, and the opportunities for employment.

We also could have explored issues of community, outlined by such social theorists as James Howard Kunstler (1996), who described the loss of connections with one another that people sense as a result of the current design of homes, subdivisions, and suburban sprawl. While those ideas may seem to be a bit of a stretch for second graders, students easily could explore the implications of homes being built without porches or what it means when neighbors cannot walk to places such as local stores. Any of these possible avenues would have made my two-day activity a more educative experience.

Toward Growth in Understanding

I continue to share this lesson as an anecdote in my classes; only now I share it for very different reasons. I offer it as an example of why teachers always should consider this important question: "How can I make my lesson *even more educative?*" While some lessons are, unfortunately, *miseducative*, it is safe to assume that most of the lessons a thoughtful teacher will generate are at least *mildly,* if not *moderately educative.* Students will learn something. The challenge, however, always should be to strive to make those lessons *even more educative.*

Dewey offers some valuable advice on how to do this. According to Dewey, an educative experience leading to growth is, foremost, based on the students' prior knowledge and experience. As teachers, we need to honor students' experiences without reducing the complexity of those experiences. In addition, we need to use prior knowledge and experience as sources of working power toward growth in understanding. As Dewey (1980, 60) noted, "We have laid it down that the educative process is a continuous process of growth, having as its aim at every stage an added capacity for growth." Further, the movement toward growth in understanding needs to be real—not contrived or driven by external, superficial reasons. "You need to know this for a test," for example, is not a legitimate justification for a truly educative experience. Whenever we separate the content of our lessons from students' experiences, impose routine for the sake of mere drill, or neglect to draw motivation from outside students' lives, we deny the educative potential of learning.

With these and other images in mind, I often ask my graduate students to develop rubrics for educative experiences that delineate *highly educative, moderately educative, minimally educative,* and *miseducative* qualities of experience. My students often keep these rubrics in the front of their lesson plan books and refer to them frequently as they reflect on their lessons. I would encourage each of you to do the same. After reading the entries related to educative experiences, try to formulate your own rubric as a tool for reflection and professional growth. With such a tool, you can confidently ask yourself, "How can I make my lessons *even more educative*?"

References

DePencier, I. B. 1967. *The history of the laboratory schools: The University of Chicago 1896–1965*. Chicago: Quadrangle Books.

Dewey, J. 1976a. *The school and society*. In *John Dewey: The middle works, 1899–1924*, ed. J. A. Boydston, Vol. 1: 1899–1901, 1–112. Carbondale, IL: Southern Illinois University Press.

Dewey, J. 1976b. *The child and the curriculum*. In *John Dewey: The middle works, 1899–1924*, ed. J. A. Boydston, Vol. 2: 1902–1903, 271–92. Carbondale, IL: Southern Illinois University Press.

Dewey, J. 1980. *Democracy and education*. In *John Dewey: The middle works, 1899–1924*, ed. J. A. Boydston, Vol. 9: 1916, 1–402. Carbondale, IL: Southern Illinois University Press.

Kunstler, J. H. 1996. *Home from nowhere: Remaking our everyday world for the twenty-first century*. New York: Simon & Schuster.

— ∽ —

Eight
The Reconstruction of Experience

Edmund C. Short

> [E]*xperiences in order to be educative must lead out into an expanding world of subject-matter. . . . This condition is satisfied only as an educator views teaching and learning as a continuous process of reconstruction of experience. . . . At every level there is an expanding development of experience if experience is educative in effect.*
> —*Experience and Education*, LW 13: 60–61

Too often we teach discrete facts or concepts that are easily ignored or soon forgotten by our students. A better approach is to conceive of our teaching as providing educative experiences. An *educative experience* is one that has the potential of being meaningfully connected to students' previous experiences and of leading to fuller, deeper understandings based on what has already been learned. The key issue for teachers creating educative experiences is to grasp what experiences students have had that can be tied into the new understandings, skills, or attitudes that are the focus of immediate curriculum aims and objectives being addressed.

Or, as Dewey (1988, 51) stated, "It thus becomes the office of the educator to select those things within the range of existing experience that have the promise and potentiality of presenting new problems which, by stimulating new ways of observing and judgment, will expand the area of further experience." Dewey (1988, 11) further noted, "Any experience is mis-educative that has the effect of arresting or distorting the growth of further experience."

Exemplifying Principles

The significance of this way of thinking lies in its two exemplifying, sound educational principles. First, we know that when students assume ownership of their learning, it is more valued, meaningful, cognitively clear, and accurate than when mental or dispositional tasks are imposed on them with little or no personal investment. Creating truly educative experiences for and with students enables them to engage such experiences with thought and emotional involvement; quick memorization and fragmented information no longer suffice as indicators of successful learning. Attention is drawn to the meaning, purpose, and interconnection of learning tasks.

Second, we know that doing one's own thinking is essential for true understanding to occur. This requires paying attention to what one has understood previously, how new information or evidence fits with or contradicts this, and how these differing understandings can be reconciled or integrated. Students must do this for themselves. A teacher cannot tell students the results or impose the answers. Each student must consider these things based on his or her own previous knowledge. Teachers can provide only the circumstances and stimulation for this educative experience to occur.

What must the nature and content of these educative experiences be? Dewey (1988, 59) wrote of the teacher providing "an expanding world of subject-matter" and of the student engaging in "a continuous process of reconstruction of experience." These components of educative experience would appear, at first glance, to be simple to spell out and enact. Yet Dewey gives few specifics on what is involved. I offer from my own years of teaching experience what I think is involved, and invite other teachers to create appropriate educative experiences for students in concrete teaching/learning situations and to share with all who are interested in truly educative experiences how these work in practice.

Attention to the Long-Range View

My interpretation of creating an educative experience includes giving careful attention to the long-range view of the subject matter. A teacher not only must see how today's lesson content fits with tomorrow's, but also with the knowledge structure of which it is a part. Teachers can plan each educative experience, leading to increasingly mature and complete understandings on the part of students, only with an accurate and comprehensive understanding of the whole subject. The trick is to select, as part of any given educative experience, the next level of content or subject matter that will allow them to build on past experience (even if but a short distance) toward attaining the fullest understanding of the subject as a whole.

Dewey (1988, 49) admitted that the "orderly development toward expansion and organization of subject-matter through growth of experience" had not received much attention by many teachers. He (1988, 57) added, "Always bear in mind, however, that intellectual organization is not an end in itself but is the means by which social relations, distinctively human ties and bonds, may be understood and more intelligently ordered." In other words, remember that even full knowledge of a subject is to be used in the service of good living, not for its own sake. How often is that being ignored today in the frantic effort to seek high test scores and mastery of bits and pieces of knowledge!

Significance to Previous Experience

Another prerequisite for creating an appropriate educative experience is to know the content and significance of the students' previous experiences related to ongoing curriculum aims and objectives. This entails careful assessment and observation of where students are in their learning. Moreover, because every student may be at a different point on the road to full understanding, a variety of next steps must be built into the subsequent educative experience. To put it bluntly, there may be no single version of an educative experience that can serve an entire class if differences in what each student needs are detected. At that point, I recommend considering the creation of individualized educative experiences for each student. Or, try creating a broad sort of educative experience—such as a project—within which each student's next step can be addressed.

For each educative experience in which students are invited to engage, teachers need to guide students by giving directions on how they should function. For instance, students will need to bring (through written or oral methods or both) what they know (or think they know) about the subject. Then, they will need to confront the next level of subject matter (through teacher talk, texts, or other media) and ask themselves, "Do I understand this in light of my personal knowledge? Does it fit in or contradict? Will I incorporate it, hold it in suspension, or do more inquiry?" At that point, students again will need to articulate their understanding (through writing or perhaps orally or both).

Guidance also must be given to students about the actual thought processes in which they engage. With regular use, students can learn what is involved in this "continuous process of reconstruction of experience," as Dewey (1988, 59) labeled it; and they can come to see that all their education involves "the progressive development of what is already experienced into a fuller and richer and also more organized form, a form that gradually approximates that in which subject-matter is presented to the skilled, mature person" (Dewey 1938, 48).

References

Dewey, J. 1988. *Experience and education*. In *John Dewey: The later works, 1925–1953*, ed. J. A. Boydston, Vol. 13: 1938–1939, 1–62. Carbondale, IL: Southern Illinois University Press.

Nine

The Relations of One Great Common World

Gary Weilbacher

> *We do not have a series of stratified earths, one of which is mathematical, another physical, another historical, and so on. We should not be able to live very long in any one taken by itself. We live in a world where all sides are bound together. All studies grow out of relations in one great common world. When the child lives in varied but concrete and active relationships to this common world, his studies are naturally unified.*
> —*The School and Society*, MW 1: 54

In theory, public schools in a democratic society are places where all sides should be bound together by the common goals of education. An educated population enhances and advances society by creating an informed, active, and caring citizenry. Seemingly, however, current educational structures are more closely aligned with sorting and stratification than with understanding relationships and promoting unity.

Curriculum Organization

The area where stratification may be most obvious is curriculum organization. Ironically, students come to school with little, if any, understanding that knowledge has been conveniently compartmentalized. They use their knowledge in an integrated manner as they try to solve problems related to their world. As students progress through the educational system, they gradually are provided with fewer opportunities to see how "all sides are bound together." Many elementary schools consist of self-contained classrooms, where one teacher, working with students grouped together because of their ages, tells them, "Now it's time to do our math lesson." Math, to the children, soon becomes a "subject" to be addressed at a particular time. To be fair, many elementary teachers teach subject knowledge by using themes related to dinosaurs and butterflies. Most students, however, begin in elementary school to understand the idea of *subjects* being separate from one another.

Even though interdisciplinary teaching is a hallmark of exemplary middle schools, such schools are few and far between. Most young adolescents see separate math, science, social studies, and language arts teachers and must make hurried choices between electives such as foreign languages, music, and art. Some middle school students are placed in algebra classes, sending the message that certain components of the discipline are more valuable than others. The result of such curricular organization is that the lines between and levels within subjects become more distinct.

Tracks

In many large high schools, students choose or are placed into general, college prep, or vocational prep tracks, where disciplines are further separated into honors, general, and remedial categories. These distinctions are further emphasized as students are separated by wings or floors within their schools. In these schools, quite clearly, groups of students are bound together because of their common characteristics, not because they share a common world.

This sorting process often is influenced by the experiential, cultural, familial, and economic backgrounds that students and teachers bring with them. Schools place differing values upon these backgrounds; students coming from less valued backgrounds learn that the skills, knowledge, and actions they used successfully in other contexts when negotiating their world are less effective in school. For many of those students, school becomes another world, distinct from the one in which they grew up. It is not overly dramatic to suggest that students who don't adjust to the school world are not "able to live very long in any one taken by itself." The large numbers of dropouts coming from less valued backgrounds provide for rather convincing evidence. On a larger scale, schools filled with students coming from impoverished conditions find themselves on "watch lists," another form of stratification indicating that such schools are not the same as achieving schools. Our educational system appears to create, foster, and value such distinctions.

Counteracting Stratification

Thus far, there seems to be little evidence to support Dewey's claims. However, the power of Dewey's words is in the possibility that any teacher can counteract the stratification imposed by the educational system, especially on a curricular and cultural level. A long, distinguished, but relatively forgotten history offers alternatives to departmentalized curriculum arrangements, including core curriculum, the project method, and arrangements created during the Eight-Year Study. These alternatives suggest that teachers do not need to teach using separate periods for individual disciplines (Aiken 1942; Hartzler 2000; Vars 1993).

Undoubtedly, such work is challenging—mainly because most teachers were not taught to teach using these ideas. Still, teachers can help their students construct "active relationships to this common world" by engaging them in curriculum planning and service learning. Teachers and students can cooperatively build curricular themes by focusing on common questions and concerns about themselves and the world around them (Beane 1997). Student concerns are steeped in cultural beliefs and reflective of the worlds in which their knowledge began to develop. Learning about these concerns does not discard the disciplines of knowledge. Rather, such learning activities "grow out of [the] relations [that are found] in one great common world." Studying such relations can reconnect the process of education with the rest of the world, especially with the students' world.

References

Aiken, W. M. 1942. *The story of the eight-year study, with conclusions and recommendations.* New York: Harper and Brothers.

Beane, J. A. 1997. *Curriculum integration: Designing the core of democratic education.* New York: Teachers College Press.

Dewey, J. 1976. *The school and society.* In *John Dewey: The middle works, 1899–1924,* ed. J. A. Boydston, Vol. 1: 1899–1901, 1–112. Carbondale, IL: Southern Illinois University Press.

Hartzler, D. S. 2000. A meta-analysis of studies conducted on integrated curriculum programs and their effects on student achievement. Unpublished doctoral diss., Indiana University, Bloomington.

Vars, G. F. 1993. *Interdisciplinary teaching: Why & how.* Columbus, OH: National Middle School Association.

— ∽ —

Ten

Learning In and Out of School: Bridging the Cultural Gap

Ron W. Wilhelm

> *From the standpoint of the child, the great waste in the school comes from his inability to utilize the experiences he gets outside the school in any complete and free way within the school itself, while, on the other hand, he is unable to apply in daily life what he is learning in school.*
> —The School and Society, MW 1: 46

Think back to your most memorable learning experience—one that continues to hold special meaning in your life. To reflect on why it was so valuable to you, consider these questions. Who was your teacher? What actions did that person take to help you learn? How did that person interact with you while you were learning? In what way was your new knowledge or skill connected to your daily life? When I have engaged adults in reflecting on these questions, they have shared that most of their truly significant learning experiences did not occur in the classroom, and most of those experiences embodied practical, life applications. How do we understand the fact that after 12 or more years of schooling, many adults point to learning experiences outside of formal education as their most memorable?

Learning involves making connections between the experienced and the possible, between the known and the imagined. Given rapidly changing demographics in U.S. schools, with increasingly culturally and linguistically diverse student populations, educators are challenged now more than ever to help students make connections and bridge cultural knowledge gaps. Much has been written over the past 30 years about the nature of school culture and the ways it can marginalize students unprepared to function in a basically middle class, white, Protestant, female classroom world. Teachers must design and build cultural bridges so that all students may connect their life experiences outside of the classroom with new knowledge, skills, and attitudes presented as part of the official curriculum. How are monocultural, monolingual teachers to take on that role?

Several practices can help educators fill their own cultural knowledge gaps and create a curriculum and learning environment that privileges student learning outside the classroom while promoting the use of new classroom knowledge in students' daily life. Consider the following questions:

- *How might I be more knowledgeable about and sensitive to students' cultural backgrounds, values, and traditions?* Teachers must be willing to confront their own misinformation, biases, and lack of cultural knowledge. The process is lifelong and involves attending to and reflecting on not only your attitudes and areas of cultural ignorance, but also on what examples you use to illustrate your lessons, what images you display on classroom walls, and what curriculum materials you select to overcome the limited or biased sources you are provided by the district.

  Though initially time-consuming, many educators begin the year with visits to their incoming students' homes. They use the visits to meet the students and parents, to answer questions about the school, and to gain insight into the home culture of each child. One important area to explore is the parents' perceptions of their own schooling experiences. Through such interaction, teachers can better understand the nature of parental involvement and support in their child's learning, and then use the information to design meaningful learning experiences grounded in the home context.

- *How do I demonstrate respect for different cultures and backgrounds in my interactions with parents and students?* Some schools organize sessions between parents and teachers to promote ongoing dialogue that focuses on educational issues of local significance. Parents can help teachers examine the norms of the local community, families, and languages for socializing children, and identify logistical barriers to parental involvement. Parents also can help teachers secure community support for the curriculum. In turn, teachers can help parents learn to engage in an ongoing dialogue with their children about learning.

- *In what ways do I provide a learning environment in which students' cultures are recognized, shared, and respected?* You can build knowledge bridges by inviting students to comment on their lives as part of the learning experience. You can give students choice and voice in the organization of learning experiences. Your challenge is to help young learners see the personal relevance of new concepts and skills. One important strategy, especially for English language learners, is to focus on how they use both their native language and English. Consider the specific ways you support the child's and family's use of their native language and how you facilitate English language development and use.

- *How do I organize opportunities for students to teach me about their cultures?* You can encourage the adventurous nature of many students by enabling them to switch roles and teach from their area of expertise, whether that be computers, sharks, or *quinceañeras* (15th birthday celebrations). Astute

41

teachers with little expertise in computer technology have engaged their students in joint learning experiences in which the students teach the teachers new computer skills.

By critically reflecting on our practice, engaging in respectful and frequent dialogue with our students and their parents, and validating students' cultural knowledge as part of the official curriculum, educators can ensure the transfer of classroom learning to life beyond the school. By traversing cultural knowledge bridges between home and school, our students will understand that knowledge and skills gained in the classroom can be used to resolve real-world problems.

Reference

Dewey, J. 1976. *The school and society.* In *John Dewey: The middle works, 1899–1924,* ed. J. A. Boydston, Vol. 1: 1899–1901, 1–112. Carbondale, IL: Southern Illinois University Press.

— ∽ —

Eleven
The Child and the Curriculum: Two Limits That Define a Single Process

William A. Reid

> *Abandon the notion of subject-matter as something fixed and ready-made in itself, outside the child's experience; cease thinking of the child's experience as also something hard and fast; see it as something fluent, embryonic, vital; and we realize that the child and the curriculum are simply two limits that define a single process.*
> —The Child and the Curriculum, MW 2: 278

Educators tend to work with simple, commonsense models of what and whom they teach. This is not to be critical of teachers. Clearly, they approach teaching this way for good reasons—the demands made upon them, their working conditions, and the need to retain their students' attention and administrators' support over the long haul. This inclination, however, typically is balanced by a degree of complexity in the teachers' visions of the point and purpose of education.

How, then, might we interpret and apply Dewey's remarks on the fluidity of the relationship between child and curriculum?

Fluent and Vital

For most of us, taking Dewey's advice too literally would be a mistake. It is all too easy to enter a classroom enthused with images of students and subject matter that are fluent and vital, only to find oneself in the midst of chaos and confusion and to end up in a state of disillusionment. Teachers in our schools are not in the enviable situation of Rousseau's (1933) tutor to Emile. Typically, they face 30 or so students of differing characters, while their choice of what to teach is restricted by school and district policies and constrained by testing programs.

An essential part of becoming a successful teacher in such circumstances is to develop an instinct for what works not just today, but next week, next month, and next year. This is what matters most where practical matters of teaching are concerned. Yet, not many teachers would be happy to operate solely on such a simplistic basis. Most feel the need for an overarching vision that helps them aspire higher in their everyday work in their classrooms. Dewey's remarks are important, therefore, because they provide such a vision in addition to offering strong links to practicality.

Practical

These links to practicality operate at two levels. First, in the right circumstances—for instance, if we were tutoring Emile—we could imagine guiding our activities so that they stimulate fluent, profoundly educative encounters between mind and subject matter. Ideally, such opportunities will, from time to time, occur in our own teaching experience. When they do, we will recognize them, know how to make use of them, and feel a sense of exhilaration as a result.

Second, Dewey's proposition has practicality outside the classroom. If, as teachers, we want to improve the nature of our practice, then Dewey can provide us with needed arguments when discussing how schooling might be improved. As noted previously, teachers tend to work with simple models of subject matter and students because of the conditions under which they teach. When debates on how these conditions might be changed arise, teachers must be influential in guiding those debates toward policies that lead to improvements in teaching.

To achieve needed change, teachers must have expertise so that they can offer solid arguments for or against particular proposals. Dewey's idea provides us with an excellent foundation for that expertise. It presents a model of learning that carries not only philosophical conviction, but also practical implications for the organization of the curriculum. As teachers, we should be able to lay out these implications with a purpose strengthened by personal experience of moments in our own classrooms when the truth of his observation manifests itself.

Reference

Dewey, J. 1976. *The child and the curriculum.* In *John Dewey: The middle works, 1899–1924,* ed. J. A. Boydston, Vol. 2: 1902–1903, 271–92. Carbondale, IL: Southern Illinois University Press.

Rousseau, J. J. 1933. *Emile.* New York: E.P. Dutton.

This photo of Dewey in academic gown at the University of Chicago was taken around 1902.

John Dewey poses with Matthias Alexander.

John Dewey portrait.

John Dewey portrait, inscribed "To my friend [?] Wang, with best regards, John Dewey, Peking, July 5, 1921."

Included among formal portraits of department heads at the University of Michigan was this one of Dewey, taken in 1893 right before he left there.

Dewey (standing, center) is photographed with the Quadrangle Club at the University of Chicago around 1896.

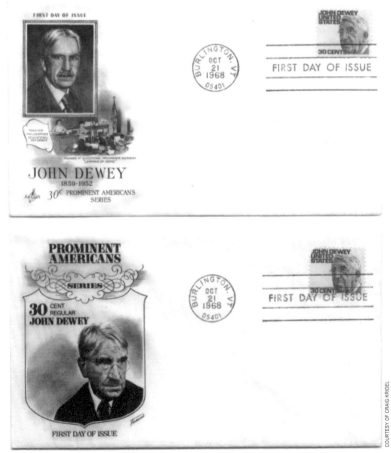

U.S. Government issued postcards.

45

Twelve
Relevance of the Curriculum

Marcella Kysilka

> *Since the curriculum is always getting loaded down with purely inherited traditional matter and with subjects which represent mainly the energy of some influential person or group of persons in behalf of something dear to them, it requires constant inspection, criticism, and revision to make sure it is accomplishing its purpose. Then there is always the probability that it represents the values of adults rather than those of children and youth, or those of pupils a generation ago rather than those of present day.*
> —*Democracy and Education*, MW 9: 250

The issue of relevance has permeated curriculum theory since its inception. What constitutes relevance is debatable among scholars in the field; however, Dewey acknowledged that curriculum always must be examined and questioned. Particularly, teachers need to ask tough questions about their curriculum. What value are these topics for the students? Why are these courses the focus of the curriculum? When was the curriculum last changed? Do all students need to have the same curriculum—particularly in secondary schools—or can the curriculum be differentiated?

Required Courses

High school curriculum in the United States has changed little in recent years. For example, most schools require students preparing for college to take a minimum of two years of mathematics. The sequence is usually Algebra I and then Geometry, because colleges and universities want students to have experience in spatial relationships, which is part of what students learn in Geometry. What makes more mathematical sense is to have Algebra I followed by Algebra II. Though Geometry could precede Algebra I or follow Algebra II, the sequence of mathematics programs in high schools remains the same as it was more than 100 years ago. Why not challenge it?

The division of mathematics into subjects such as Algebra I and II, Geometry, Pre-Algebra, Trigonometry, Calculus, and Analytic Geometry is an artificial one. In many countries, mathematics is not divided into separate subjects, but is simply referred to as "maths." Students receive the same content as students in the United States, likely at a more rigorous level. What exactly is Pre-Algebra? How does that differ from general mathematics or even Algebra, and why is that course in the curriculum? When mathematics is divided into separate courses, what students miss the most in their study is the interconnectedness between ideas and the understanding of mathematics as a field of study. The division has no academic meaning; it is simply a convenience for schools and a way to communicate to parents about their children's achievement level. In communications with parents, "Pre-Algebra" certainly sounds more academic than "mathematics."

Other areas of the curriculum also need to be examined and questioned. Why is social studies taught as separate courses in Political Science, History, Economics, and Geography? Can students really study history without understanding the politics and economic conditions of the time, as well as the geographical relationships between countries? The English curriculum begs similar questions. English is taught by geographic areas—American Literature, World Literature, and British Literature—without consideration for how these pieces of literature are related. Does it make sense to study British authors without considering what American authors were writing during the same period and whether the ideas have any relationship or were influenced by what was happening politically? Moreover, why is literature often separated from writing? Can students study grammar and composition without reading anything?

Another question deals with what constitutes the "literature" in English classes. Why are the selections there? Do students read *Romeo and Juliet* in 10th grade because they might "connect" and empathize with the characters, who are about their age? What relevance is their plight to that of the readers? How many generations of students need to read *Catcher in the Rye?* Has another book been written that could convey the same message to young readers? The literature in English classes is rarely questioned, yet many students find English boring and irrelevant. Perhaps they are bored because they do not see the purpose of reading the required books and short stories that make up the curriculum.

Like the sequences for mathematics, social studies, and English, the science curriculum also is problematic in high schools. What is the rationale for the sequence of Earth Science, Biology, Physics, and Chemistry? Though many science teachers believe that this is not necessarily the best sequence, it hasn't changed in years. What are the ramifications of students taking Chemistry before Physics or Biology before Earth Science? For that matter, why do all students have to take these classes rather than study Botany, Marine Science, or Space?

Student Input

What is so essential about the current secondary curriculum that we are afraid to change it? Today's curriculum is based on tradition and assumptions. First, the curriculum assumes a body of students who plan to go on to postsecondary experiences. Second, the existing curriculum is designed to prepare students for high-stakes tests they are required to pass to graduate from high school. Seemingly, then, the current curriculum is irreplaceable.

The important message in Dewey's remarks lies in the last few lines of the preceding quote. In essence, Dewey is saying that the curriculum, when examined, is done so by adults who either stick with tradition or make adjustments to meet some outside influence. No one seems to think to ask students what they want or need to learn. Perhaps we are afraid that students will make poor choices. We should consider the possibility that, given a chance, students might decide on content that is much more challenging than what we provide for them. Students might even suggest that the same curriculum is not appropriate for all learners. Perhaps they, better than we, know what they want and need. If students have input into what they will learn, relevance may no longer be such a debated issue for academics.

Reference

Dewey, J. 1980. *Democracy and education.* In *John Dewey: The middle works, 1899–1924,* ed. J. A. Boydston, Vol. 9: 1916, 1–402. Carbondale, IL: Southern Illinois University Press.

— ∽ —

Thirteen
Two Approaches to Planning

William Van Til

> The traditional scheme is, in essence, one of imposition from above
> and from outside. It imposes adult standards, subject matter, and methods
> upon those who are only growing slowly toward maturity. The gap is so
> great that the required subject matter, the methods of learning and of
> behaving are foreign to the existing capacities of the young.
> —*Experience and Education,* LW 13: 6

As a young teacher-to-be, I rejected "imposition from above and from outside." But how to proceed? I took two variant approaches to planning subject matter and methodology with high school students in the Ohio State University School. The first was in my first year of teaching at the University School; the second came nine years later. Each is described in greater detail in my autobiography, *My Way of Looking at It* (1996, chapters 15 and 21).

Student-Determined Subject Matter

After my liberal arts education at Columbia College, I taught for a year in a New York State reform school that had no books, no materials, no courses of study—but plenty of juvenile delinquents. So among my very first classes at the experimental University School was a two-hour block of time for teaching a dozen sophomore and junior boys whom the faculty perceived as "having problems." I began with extended self-introductions by both the boys and myself. Then, because I knew little more about education at the age of 23 than that learning must be based on the needs and interests of the learner, I asked flatly what they wanted to learn about. One boy assumed group leadership and spoke out to test me, "We want to learn all about crooks. Is that all right with you, Mr. Van Til?" His followers supported him. I was at a crossroad; I could stand pat or I could scuttle. I said, "What do you want to know about crooks?" The leader answered, "Where do the crooks live?" His followers had additional questions. Because I did know that teachers gave assignments, I told them to ask their parents that night where the crooks in Columbus lived.

The next morning, they reported that their parents didn't know where the crooks lived. Several students urged, "Let's ask the cops." Again I was at a crossroad. We were mobile because several had cars and we had two hours of class time. So we piled into cars and went to the police station. The desk sergeant showed us entries on the police blotter and took us on a tour of the cells. The following morning, the boys pointed out indignantly, "That dumb cop didn't tell us where the crooks lived; he just showed where crimes were committed. Doesn't anybody know?"

I did some homework and learned of several dissertations, which had been sponsored by a campus sociology professor, on the social problems of Columbus. As a class, we went to the university library and checked out several dissertations and other references on crime. The boys copied many of the maps and charts. But these were young men of action. "Let's go see." We did. "Let's tell others" about these multiple problem areas. So they took many photographs in the Columbus areas in which most social problems concentrated.

Back at school the science teacher helped the students develop their pictures and taught them some science in the process. The fine arts teacher taught them about lettering and chart making. I helped with composition, reading difficulties, and writing problems. When the maps and charts were completed, the question of where and how to display them arose. The University School librarian controlled the school's display cases and, as a condition of use, required the boys to include books on crime and reviews of the books. The boys rightly suspected me of plotting with the librarian. Yet they followed her instructions on how to use the Dewey decimal system. They withdrew relevant books on crime, read within the books, and prepared written reviews and summaries for the showcases.

When the exhibits went up, the boys got positive feedback from students, faculty, and even some parents. I felt encouraged as I reviewed in my mind the social science concepts, scientific generalizations, art experiences, substantial reading and writing of the past weeks, new interests developed by the boys, and their positive recognition by the school. The crime study readily led into a study of housing in Columbus and the nation. During one visit to a housing project, a well-informed African-American man was our guide. On the way back to school, one of my boys said, "You know why he's so smart? Because he's got white blood. Isn't that right, Mr. Van Til?" "Let's look it up," I said. During the next several weeks, we learned about race and racial relations in Columbus and the wider world.

Jointly Determined Subject Matter

Nine years later, I taught my last classes at the University School. By then I had a master's degree in civic education from Columbia's Teachers College and was nearing my doctoral degree in curriculum at The Ohio State University after studying with OSU's stars Boyd H. Bode, Harold Alberty, H. Gordon Hullfish, and Louis Raths. I also had learned from my University School colleagues, including H. H. (Mike) Giles and Lou LaBrant. (Mike was once asked a hostile question by a conference attendant: "Mr. Giles, in the title of your book, *Teacher-*

Pupil Planning [1941], which is most important—teacher or pupil?" Without hesitation, Mike responded, "The hyphen.")

By then I had learned that in planning, teachers and students could jointly develop criteria by which the worth of proposed topics and problems could be judged. As a teacher, I could freely suggest and support criteria and content reflecting my philosophy of education. I believed in meeting the personal and social needs of learners, throwing light on social realities, and clarifying and advancing democratic values. Students would be heard and respected, their criteria considered, and their content proposals generally adopted.

In the nine hours weekly of the last core program I taught at the University School, the high school senior class with its team of teachers developed criteria to apply to proposed topics and problems of study. The senior class, graduating into a 1943 world at war, chose to study the background of the current conflict, military service, civil defense, war industry, economics, and international organization for the coming postwar period.

Early in the ten weeks devoted to the topic and problem of postwar planning, they read books and pamphlets, listened to guest lecturers, and heard recordings. Then they developed a list of 91 possible postwar problems. Each student wrote an essay titled "What Am I Fighting For and Against?" They researched possible alternatives for the American economy, proposed international organizations, participated in heated panel discussions, and wrote their individual conclusions. For background, the brightest student read six scholarly books and seven pamphlets, while the slowest student read one entire pamphlet and excerpts from five others.

Committees were formed to present recommendations on the economy and on international organization to the class. The recommendations were voted on, and the agreed-upon proposals were sent to key members of the U.S. Congress and other influential people. Among the responses received was one from Eleanor Roosevelt, who wrote, "the important thing is that those young people are learning to think constructively and, though many of them may think differently in a few years, they have the ability to grow."

Two Possible Approaches

Over the many years that followed, I often have thought about which was the better of these two approaches to planning subject matter and methodology with high school students. What do you think about these two approaches to planning? How are they similar? How are they different? How can we best avoid "imposition from above and from outside"?

Reference

Dewey, J. 1988. *Experience and education*. In *John Dewey: The later works, 1925–1953*, ed. J. A. Boydston, Vol. 13: 1938–1939, 1–62. Carbondale, IL: Southern Illinois University Press.

Giles, H. H. 1941. *Teacher-pupil planning*. New York: Harper.

Van Til, W. 1996. *My way of looking at it: An autobiography*, 2nd ed. revised and expanded. San Francisco: Caddo Gap Press.

— ∽ —

Fourteen
What Imposed Standards Do to the Child

M. Frances Klein

> *The source of whatever is dead, mechanical, and formal in schools is found precisely in the subordination of the life and experience of the child to the curriculum.*
> —The Child and the Curriculum, MW 2: 277

This is a time when standards that set levels of expectations and define excellence in many areas are being established for American education. We have, for example, standards for students to meet in various content areas, high-stakes tests that set standards for achievement, textbooks that meet selection criteria, and specific learning expectations that direct how time is to be spent in the classroom. On the surface, finding fault with having high teacher and student standards is difficult. Who can oppose this drive for excellence in education? The issue of what educational standards to have must be carefully considered, however, because of the significant impact they can have on the lives of students. The issue is further complicated by the fact that not all standards are in agreement with one another.

In spite of the many claims to the contrary, the impact of many of the current standards on student learning has not been positive. Many students are compliant about school requirements and work hard to meet these formal expectations. Others question expectations and sometimes seek other means of education that are not so rigidly controlled. Some students simply drop out of school because it no longer seems relevant to them. In light of Dewey's observation, we should carefully examine how these imposed standards affect student learning in at least three areas: the isolation of evaluation from the ongoing work of the classroom and the curriculum; the curriculum imbalance that results from the imposition of current standards; and the restriction of learning materials to the textbook. These conditions have led to excesses and bad educational practices.

Isolation of Evaluation

High-stakes tests are the dominant form of evaluation in most states. They have removed evaluation as an inherent component of teaching and learning processes. The proper role of evaluation (in various forms)—as a means to determine what students have learned and to suggest what next steps might be warranted for particular students—is missing. It has been replaced by standards set far afield from the classroom and the use of standardized tests as the dominant form of evaluation. In the final analysis, this form of evaluation is the only one that counts.

Students in my own community, for example, are coached on how to take standardized tests, subjected to pep rallies to get them revved up to do their best on high-stakes tests, treated to breakfast at school on the day of testing, given sugar snacks just before testing, and presented with gift certificates to stores in the local mall when they do well on the state tests. Ongoing evaluations as a part of the educational process are ignored in favor of what must be done to get lagging or failing students up to grade level or beyond for the next round of high-stakes tests. Teachers feel a keen sense of what they must do to prepare students for the state tests, because the rewards are dependent upon scores the students make on the mandated tests.

Curriculum Imbalance

The curriculum students experience in the classroom has been seriously out of balance for many years. This phenomenon is a significant result of the student's role being severely diminished as the drive for high standards becomes more dominant. (Unfortunately, budgetary constraints also have been a factor.) Time spent in elementary schools to get students up to standards in reading and math has too often limited the curriculum to little else except those two areas. In the push to meet standards, the arts, social studies, and science have received short shrift or even have been eliminated from the curriculum; and the impact on the quality of schooling as described by Dewey has been eliminated from discussions about curriculum. Few of us would recognize this condition as a desirable feature of the education we want for our students.

Restricted Learning Materials

Though textbooks have been judged as severely limited by a variety of studies, the curriculum—planned and implemented to meet high standards—has strengthened the use of a single textbook in classrooms. Students whose interests may be beyond what is between the covers of the text are not encouraged to explore other topics, nor are teachers rewarded for trying to make the curriculum more responsive to students' needs and interests by using a variety of learning materials. Supplemental materials that might make the curriculum more interesting, understandable, and relevant to the lives of students are not found in many classrooms. The textbook that best matches the high-stakes tests becomes the only teaching and learning tool to be found. This situation severely restricts the curriculum and disregards the students' interests in the learning process.

Our schools must be able to give evidence of what is being taught by teachers and learned by students. New ways to foster excellence in American education—beyond the remotely and politically set standards that do not take into account students' needs and interests—are desperately needed. Though many teachers continue to do all they can to honor the lives and experiences of students beyond the classroom as they work within the designated curriculum, their work is severely handicapped by the drive to meet high external standards. We have overlooked a significant part of the equation for school success: the student and what he or she brings to school today. Dewey's reflection on "the source of whatever is dead, mechanical, and formal in schools" as stemming from "the subordination of the life and experience of the child to the curriculum" is just as applicable today as when he first penned it.

Reference

Dewey, J. 1976. *The child and the curriculum*. In *John Dewey: The middle works, 1899–1924*, ed. J. A. Boydston, Vol. 2: 1902–1903, 271–92. Carbondale, IL: Southern Illinois University Press.

— ∽ —

Fifteen
How Mechanization Leads to Contempt for the Teaching and Learning Process

Louise Anderson Allen

> *Familiarity breeds contempt, but it also breeds something like affection. We get used to the chains we wear, and we miss them when they are removed. . . . It is possible for the mind to develop interest in a routine or mechanical procedure if conditions are continually supplied which demand that mode of operation and preclude any other sort.*
> —The Child and the Curriculum, MW 2: 288

What chains impede teachers in creating learning environments? We may readily identify restrictions on a continuum of enforcement from those imposed by dictatorial administrators to the ones now mandated by the federal No Child Left Behind legislation. Most teachers are well aware of how they are tied by both federal and state accountability requirements through the chains of the mechanical procedures of a standardized curriculum or a standard course of study. Other chains, however, are equally binding and far more insidious.

Indeed, most teachers are used to, comfortable with, and perhaps complacent about what has become the most common of all chains that bind them to the standard operating procedure in many American classrooms—canned curricula that are pervasive and that demand a far more mechanized approach to the teaching and learning process. How do teachers come to know and accept these chains they are first forced to wear and eventually may embrace as a well-loved friend?

Canned Curricula

These curricula—used in nearly every subject matter and discipline—have bound teachers and their students to others' thoughts, methods, and teachings. Teachers have developed such an overreliance on them that they do not seek freedom from mindlessness or the freedom found in the flexibility in planning, creating, and participating in learning experiences. In fact, many teachers voice much affection for the canned curricula that help them make it through the day with students who seem unmotivated and uninterested in classroom lessons. Canned curricula represent the strongest and tightest links in the chains that bind education to standardization and mechanization.

If education is to provide educative experience as Dewey intended, then teachers first must recognize the chains beyond the state and federal mandates that are immediate to their environment. Teachers use canned curricula that have little or no relationship or relevance for students who sit in classrooms day after day participating in a routine that fosters thoughtlessness. These curricula are a part of the mechanization that places teachers in the position of being merely deliverers of information that is perceived by students as meaningless. How can we change this situation? What conditions must be in place in schools that will encourage a nonmechanistic view of the teaching and learning process? Whose role is it to ensure that teachers and students do not develop contempt for school, but through a respect for education learn to understand and desire the reciprocity of the teaching and learning process?

Breaking out of the Mechanistic Routine

These are the challenges faced by all educators today in our public schools. Principals and superintendents are under tremendous pressure for schools to meet state and federal guidelines on standardized tests. They, in turn, place an equal amount of pressure on teachers and students, who then must perform to someone else's standards. In each instance, educators become part of a mechanistic routine that breeds familiarity and contempt for the teaching and learning process. Students are no longer performing to their own best ability, but to someone else's definition of what is standard for some mythical average student somewhere in the middle of Nowhere, USA.

While this situation may seem hopeless, teachers can reclaim their role by breaking these chains. One of the greatest joys and most profound responsibilities of being a teacher is that of creating new ideas, new learning situations, and new materials in response to the needs of students. Teachers are role models for students as learners. If teachers are enchained to a mechanistic view of learning, then students never will have role models in their classrooms to teach them how to be thinkers and analyzers. In this mechanization of the curricula, chains develop and familiarity sets in, leading to contempt for the teaching and learning process. But if teachers are urged by school leaders and officials to move away from learning experiences that numb the mind and limit student learning, then they will serve as the kind of role models we claim we want for students.

Creating Critical Thinkers

If we want students to think and analyze critically, then we must want that for teachers as well. Accordingly, teachers should not be chained to canned curricula but provided with opportunities to learn how to develop curricula appropriate for their students. Furthermore, school leaders and teachers should create learning opportunities for students to experience learning from one another and teaching one another, including opportunities for teachers and school leaders to serve in the student role. In this way, the teacher-student relationship will be shown not simply as one situated in a power relationship, but in the love of learning. This approach should provide all participants with evidence that the teaching and learning process is one that does not have to lead to standardization, but one that is constantly being reinvented and reinvigorated by the participants—the teachers and the students.

Reference

Dewey, J. 1976. *The child and the curriculum*. In *John Dewey: The middle works, 1899–1924*, ed. J. A. Boydston, Vol. 2: 1902–1903, 271–92. Carbondale, IL: Southern Illinois University Press.

— ∽ —

Sixteen
The Teacher-Artist

George Willis

> *Until the artist is satisfied in perception with what he is doing, he continues shaping and reshaping. The making comes to an end when its result is experienced as good—and that experience comes not by mere intellectual and outside judgment but in direct perception. An artist, in comparison with his fellows, is one who is not only especially gifted in powers of execution but in unusual sensitivity to the qualities of things. This sensitivity also directs his doings and makings.*
> —Art as Experience, LW 10: 56

Despite the deep philosophic ideas John Dewey discussed throughout his writings and the careful, scholarly tone he invariably took, his philosophy can be described as "naturalistic"—that is, his primary concern was not with abstract matters, but with how people actually cope with the basic problems of living. In this sense, he is like a conscientious parent, always reminding us about situations we have lived through that we did not quite understand at the time, always hoping that we will not need his reminders in the future.

The passage cited is not an exception. In it, he insisted that you, as a teacher, are an artist. Furthermore, you must remember that each of your students is an artist, too. This observation may not be one you made as you embarked on your teaching career—especially given the emphasis American society now places on technological solutions to all problems, even educational ones—but it is an observation that Dewey insisted you make. And he was right to insist. You are not an artist because Dewey said you are, but because artistry is at the heart of what being a thoughtful teacher is all about. Indeed, artistry is an essential part of all thoughtful, moral living.

Aesthetic Experience

Dewey insisted again and again in his writings that teachers as artists are necessarily reflective practitioners—constantly sizing up the multitude of newly arising situations in their classrooms, seeking and weighing appropriate evidence, making value judgments, and taking practical actions. As a teacher, you want to do all this well. But how?

Though Dewey often used the word "science" to describe the public side of reflection, he made clear (especially in his later writings, such as the passage cited) that the private side, rooted in personal experience, is more important. Reflective teaching is primarily aesthetic; any utilitarian concerns about what specifics students may or may not have learned, however important, are secondary. You, as a teacher, are inevitably a teacher-artist. You can become a better teacher-artist only through deepening your own aesthetic experience, refining your ability to perceive that which is not obvious, and acting on your perceptions in creative ways that help others to perceive the world anew, more clearly and more intensely.

And how is all this done? As the old joke puts it, the lost musician, carrying a violin case, constantly glancing at his watch, and frantically scurrying along mid-Manhattan streets, finally asks a passerby, "Can you tell me how to get to Carnegie Hall?" The reply: "Practice, practice, practice."

Direct Perceptions

You still may find all this difficult to believe. After all, aren't teachers teachers because they help students learn what they need to know? Of course! Except, as Dewey often pointed out, no one can say with certainty exactly what any one person—let alone everyone—needs to lead a personally fulfilling and socially useful life. Therefore, teachers must rely on their direct perceptions of what goes on in their classrooms to make their own choices about what activities to suggest to students and about how to shape the environment within which each student lives. There is simply no other way to discern the intensely personal reactions of students.

The process is ongoing. It can come to a halt (and then only temporarily—unlike many other forms of art) only when the teacher-artist stops to reflect on it. Remembering that "good" is both an aesthetic and an ethical term, the teacher can stop and say about what is going on in his or her classroom, "I feel this to be good. I believe this to be good. I will try in the future to create something even better, but for the moment this will do."

The Creative Process

Furthermore, you must not lose sight of the fact that your students, too, are artists. What goes on in your classroom is not solely your creation. You must, therefore, involve your students in the creative process, the perceiving, the doing, the shaping, the reshaping—all that goes into making the classroom what it is. There are many ways to do this. You can work out many artistic techniques in your own classroom. You and other teacher-artists in your school, or even throughout the world, can work out and share specifics. Such sharing has been going on for years, and it is now easier than ever. Your students will be glad to help, especially when they understand that their own doings and makings are valued artistic endeavors.

So, as Dewey reminded us, perception heightens sensitivity. Sensitivity heightens awareness. Awareness increases attention to not only what is, but to all the possibilities of what can be. In our present era, one that denigrates the essential aesthetic and moral value of teaching, persevere in what Dewey knew and all perceptive teachers know to be true. Don't let your identity as a teacher-artist be taken away from you.

Reference

Dewey, J. 1987. *Art as experience*. In *John Dewey: The later works, 1925–1953,* ed. J. A. Boydston, Vol. 10: 1934, 1–456. Carbondale, IL: Southern Illinois University Press.

Seventeen
Effort: The Outgrowth of Individual Interest

Robert C. Morris

> *If the subject-matter of the lessons be such as to have an appropriate place within the expanding consciousness of the child, if it grows out of his own past doings, thinkings, and sufferings, and grows into application in further achievements and receptivities, then no device or trick of method has to be resorted to in order to enlist 'interest.' The psychologized is of interest—that is, it is placed in the whole of conscious life so that it shares the worth of that life.*
> —The Child and the Curriculum, MW 2: 288

As a young educator beginning my career in 1970, I quickly came to realize that finding and developing the interests of my students was paramount if I wanted to be successful. Identifying the appropriate teaching experiences that would begin the process for student involvement and interest is where many of my early struggles were focused. Like many aspiring teachers, I saw my task as clearly that of directing my students toward a given end, such as getting the correct answer or scoring high on a test. But therein likely would be found my greatest early weakness. Instead of "directing," I should have been only "facilitating" my students toward their own given ends. Student interest, as I have come to see it, is not teacher interest, nor parent interest, but truly must be student interest.

Know Your Students

By identifying and focusing on each individual student and his or her own driving interests and desires, teachers and even parents have a much better chance of not only reaching students, but also of understanding them. Knowing your own students has to be the beginning point. Recognizing things about each student that make up his or her world and understandings is an essential ingredient. This is not to say that one is restricted, as Dewey (1976, 288) noted, "to the chains we wear," but only to understanding those chains each student brings, and maybe how these chains affect each student. For students, these chains could be socioeconomic, geographic, or any number of other restrictive elements.

Knowing where a student is "coming from" is an important first criterion for developing interest. Naturally, to find out about your students, you have to investigate and search. Asking questions is a beginning. Inquiry also must be a continuous activity, especially as your students grow and develop. As a teacher, I'm always pleased to see the interests of my students increase and expand over a period of time. Seeing former students and finding out where their own interests took them over a lifetime always has been intriguing to me.

Identify Pertinent Subject Matter

A second criterion for developing student interest has to do with clearly identifying pertinent subject matter. Looking for appealing and appropriate curricular and instructional activities is essential. I have come to believe that keeping students on task and focused is not that difficult to do, as long as I've done my homework. When I have found appealing subject matter that fits nicely with the learning experiences I'm creating, students usually are on task.

Consider the Environment

I'm not exactly sure when something that is found appealing turns into something "interesting," but the concept of making things agreeable rather than disagreeable is, no doubt, a motivational factor. Like the subject matter, the environment also should be agreeable. The environment or setting is a third criterion for developing student interest. From both a psychological and sociological standpoint, the school's environment can be monumental in its effect on a child. Imagine a classroom where students are not challenged nor stimulated, where instructors are mechanical in nature or, worse yet, on a video or being telecast with no possible interaction. Though a lot rides on teacher-directed activity, a school's overall environment and the individual atmosphere of each classroom are factors to consider when developing student interest.

Of course, for Dewey, the end result of student interest was "action" on the part of the student. I tend to favor his later use of the term "effort" as the outgrowth of individual interest. Effort put forth by students truly interested in the idea or activity they are investigating has always been my realization of the Dewey quote cited. Effort seems to represent the final and end result of individual interest; and effort best asserts Dewey's concept of the complete experience for the child.

Reference

Dewey, J. 1976. *The child and the curriculum.* In *John Dewey: The middle works, 1899–1924,* ed. J. A. Boydston, Vol. 2: 1902–1903, 271–92. Carbondale, IL: Southern Illinois University Press.

Eighteen
Growth: The Consummate Open-Ended Aspiration

Paul Shaker

> *We have laid it down that the educative process is a continuous process*
> *of growth, having as its aim at every stage an added capacity of growth.*
> —*Democracy and Education*, MW 9: 54

Our greatest sages leave us not only with a legacy of clarity and insight, but also with enigma. As their reflections on life reach the limits of expression, we often are left with claims that transcend language and logic. Such ideas may appear mystical, repetitive, or vague. They are attempts to stretch current language and concepts to offer an understanding of the emerging world. Though such writing may attract the ridicule of contemporaries, it carries quite a different meaning to those who come later. These concepts may become the authors' principal legacy and the reason for their lasting recognition. "Every event in the visible world is the effect of an 'image,'" states the *I Ching* (in Wilhelm 1967, vii). Those whose writing reaches across time seek to design those images.

From ancient times, Plato's Theory of Forms can be seen in this light, foreshadowing Gestalt and certain other schools of psychology that have a structural bent. Two millennia after they were spoken, the Beatitudes of the Sermon on the Mount enunciate spiritual values and a way of life that remain beyond the grasp of all but a few Christians. Buddha's Four Noble Truths also fit this description of a life practice few can adopt or explain, but which constellates an ideal. In the 19th century, the Romantic Poets and Walt Whitman described sublime states and heightened consciousness. In the 20th century, C. G. Jung coined terms such as "archetype" and "synchronicity" in an attempt to bring science to the mysteries of the human mind. At the same time, John Dewey extended the traditions of the Transcendentalists and American Pragmatists by putting forward his concept of "growth."

Growth as a Metaphor

In its many formulations, Dewey's statements about "growth" typically are marked by their circularity. Growth is described as the aim of life and defined as a continuous process. Truly educative experience is that which leads to further education and growing. Education has as its aim an added capacity for growth. Though the concept of growth is pivotal to Dewey, he nonetheless repeatedly portrayed it in such puzzling ways. Stylistically, this is not the Dewey to which we are accustomed. Typically, he is a paragon of logic and conventional scientific thought, a consummate rationalist. In the treatment of growth, his central metaphor, he steps out of character with statements that resemble Zen koans more than they do syllogisms. Perhaps in this instance, Dewey sought to touch something that lies beyond the reach of his normal philosopher's tools.

On one level, Dewey alerted us to the significance of change by employing a familiar natural metaphor to redirect thinking on education toward process rather than product. Dewey subverted traditional thinking about education and its emphasis on "acquiring knowledge" by presenting a central aim that is content-less, open-ended, ineffable, and emerging. Today's lesson can be evaluated only in terms of what happens to the student tomorrow, not what the student "knows" today. A course of study, degree, or program has value in terms of whether graduates go forward into life, striving for further development as a result of their education.

And on those tomorrows, when we look back and try to determine through our current achievements whether the education we have received has been of merit, our answer will be determined by yet another tomorrow's achievements. The process has no end, not even death, because our influence can survive us as has Dewey's. All our evaluation is formative, not summative. Even the best ideas often become obsolete and a burden on future society, because they are valued for their past effects rather than their current impact. The cost of stasis gives emphasis to the need for a constructive attitude toward change and growth.

> *The old order changeth, yielding place to new,*
> *And God fulfills himself in many ways,*
> *Lest one good custom should corrupt the world.*
> —Alfred Tennyson (1863, line 408)

Accommodating Chance

Through his concept of growth, Dewey also equiped us with a way to accommodate chance. Though in our Western tradition we construct elaborate plans that are in turn executed by the application of technology and the exercise of will, we are not impervious to the results of chance. An act of nature, an airplane crash, or a virus can appear without warning and topple our well-laid plans. If the world is a fully predictable place, decoded by cause and effect, we have not yet fully found a way to break that code. Jung offered the maligned or ignored concept of synchronicity as an explanation. In the absence of such explanations, much of what we experience still has the air of chance, coincidence, or even chaos. Dewey's formulation of growth does not demystify chance. Instead, it provides a method of coping with phenomena that are beyond our ability to control or predict. Dewey's "growth" gives us a means of responding to the unforeseen. This guiding principle allows us to encounter the great reversals of life and emerge with our psyches, if not our families or fortune, intact. The great stories of survival and triumph against adversity are applications of Dewey's concept of growth.

> *Everything, even life, is eventually taken away from you. You cannot feel, cannot touch its expression. You can only reach its reflection. If you try to grasp happiness itself your fingers only meet a surface of glass, because happiness has no existence of its own.*
> —Douglas Sirk (1959)

Transformation

Dewey's idea of growth is, however, more than a way of rationalizing fate and coping with the unforeseen. Ultimately, he has by his formulation not only opened the possibility of, but also put an emphasis on transformation. "Growth" in this sense is the consummate open-ended aspiration. No static state of perfection, bliss, competence, or control is postulated as a goal. Rather, Dewey invites those who would be educated to join in a noncyclic, unending process of living. Implicit in this address to life is perseverance because, by definition, the process is ongoing and ends for the individual only with the end of consciousness.

As I go through life and reflect on this principle of Dewey with the benefit of greater experience and maturity, I increasingly appreciate its genius. I feel that I cannot truly grasp the idea of life as a continuous unfolding—that I am touching a "surface of glass" (Sirk 1959) when I attempt to do so. Yet, as time goes by, increasingly I have intimations of the truth of this assertion. Each moment of every day, we are challenged to integrate the experiences that come to us. Living is defined in these encounters, and the quality of our lives is so determined. Each day, we rise to meet the challenges and gifts living presents us; and, as day ends, we can take stock in a transitory way of whether the capacity for growth in us has been preserved and transformed.

Reference

Dewey, J. 1980. *Democracy and education*. In *John Dewey: The middle works, 1899–1924*, ed. J. A. Boydston, Vol. 9: 1916, 1–402. Carbondale, IL: Southern Illinois University Press.

Sirk, D., director. 1959. *Imitation of life*. DVD. Santa Monica, CA: Universal Music and Video Distribution, 2003.

Tennyson, A. 1863. The passing of Arthur. In *Idylls of the king*. Boston: Ticknor and Fields.

Wilhelm, R. 1967. *The I Ching*. Princeton, NJ: Princeton University Press.

— ✁ —

PART III
CRITICAL
THINKING

The 'Varied and Unusual' Abuses of Critical Thinking

Donna Adair Breault

As a second-year teacher, I sat in the media center ready for an afternoon staff development seminar. An outside consultant was coming in to teach us "Talents," a critical thinking curriculum. From what I can recall 15 years later, there were five "talents" that we were to teach our students. While I cannot remember them exactly, I know that one dealt with planning, another with brain-storming, and one involved predicting problems; the two remaining fell suit in some similar fashion regarding the depth of thought involved. What I do re-member quite clearly, however, was the "teacher talk" that the consultant drilled into our heads that day.

"Teachers, can you think of the many *varied* and *unusual* uses for this button?" the consultant asked as she held up a simple black button. The manner in which she drew out the terms "varied" and "unusual" immediately indicated their im-portance within the program. Teachers spent the next few minutes brainstorm-ing uses for the button with varying degrees of engagement. Following a defini-tion and discussion of brainstorming, the consultant proceeded to share pictures students had made demonstrating the varied and unusual uses of the button; then she reinforced the need to use the "teacher talk" we would be given as part of the program. "There needs to be consistency from grade level to grade level," the consultant contended, "so you always need to ask for 'varied and unusual uses' of objects when conducting a brainstorming activity."

Prescribed Lessons

As I looked around the room, I was surprised that I did not see physical signs from any of the teachers that they too recognized the irony in our experience that day. Finally, annoyed by the whole experience, I spoke up. "Isn't it a bit ironic that you are giving us a prescribed script to teach children to think critically?" My question was met with harsh glances from my administrators and countless protests from the consultant. The seminar continued without question. As duti-ful teachers, we took our "Talents" curriculum to our classrooms and immedi-ately began to implement it. Before long, you could see bulletin board displays up and down the hall: "Varied and Unusual Uses for a Button," "Varied and Unusual Uses for a Spoon," "Varied and Unusual Uses for a Tire," and the list went on and on.

Throughout my nine years of teaching, I saw a number of critical thinking curricula come and go, and unfortunately most were not much better than my first exposure to "Talents." Most were skill-based with prescribed lessons; and throughout them all, I marveled at the irony that surrounded my life as a teacher: "How can you expect me to teach critical thinking when you don't allow me to think critically as a professional?"

Nurturing Thinking

Once I became an administrator, I was in a position to build professional development that would promote critical thinking. To plan the professional development, I had to stop and seriously think about some important questions: "What is critical thinking? Is it something that can be taught? If so, how do we teach teachers to teach it?" Faced with these and other questions, I turned to two valuable resources—a trusted colleague and Dewey.

Based on my readings of Dewey, I believe that critical thinking is an inherent capacity to be nurtured and developed. The "skills" that seem to be the focus of so much of the critical thinking curricula I had known may be instrumentalities to aid in critical thinking, but in and of themselves are not critical thinking. To delineate them as such is like confusing the bow and arrow for the goal of shooting a target. Dewey (1980, 112) made this analogy:

> But we must remember that the object is only a mark or sign by which the mind specifies the activity one desires to carry out. Strictly speaking, not the target but hitting the target is the end in view. . . . The different objects which are thought of are means of directing activity.

With this in mind, I also considered other things I had read from Dewey regarding the nature of critical thinking to determine what was needed in the professional development experience: a sense of mental unrest (1978), real opportunities to engage the learner to solve relevant problems (1984), encouragement for playful consideration of possibilities (1976a; 1976b), challenges to suspend judgment (1978), and hopes for even the "audacity of imagination" (1984, 247).

Conversations with Teachers

Using these images, my trusted colleague and I planned and implemented the critical thinking professional development. The half-day sessions looked very different from what I had experienced as a teacher. Instead of prescribed materials, we had conversations with teachers. We also offered relevant, though fun, situations in which the teachers themselves had to think critically to solve problems. We offered images from the past, such as the life and work of Leonardo da Vinci; and we explored images from film that captured moments of incredible problem solving, such as the scene from *Apollo 13* when the scientists were trying to find a way to create breathing apparatuses for the astronauts from the materials they knew were on the capsule.

From there, we discussed ways teachers could alter what they were doing in their classrooms to foster higher levels of critical thinking, and we continued the conversations after I or the teachers attempted the various lessons in the classrooms. Ultimately, my colleague and I were trying to help teachers see their work differently—to begin to think critically about their work as teachers so they could, in turn, help students think more critically about their work.

While I cannot claim to have achieved a pinnacle in professional development in my work with teachers that year, I do believe it was a fairly significant step in the right direction, and certainly a more meaningful experience than the afternoon staff development I had endured as a teacher years earlier. I hope that when you read the contributions in this section regarding critical thinking, you too will develop significant images of its potential in your work. While your definition may not be identical to the one I have outlined here, the fact that you are developing that image is in itself a significant act of critical thinking and a wonderful opportunity for your own professional development.

References

Dewey, J. 1976a. *The school and society*. In *John Dewey: The middle works, 1899–1924*, ed. J. A. Boydston, Vol. 1: 1899–1901, 1–112. Carbondale, IL: Southern Illinois University Press.

Dewey, J. 1976b. *The child and the curriculum*. In *John Dewey: The middle works, 1899–1924*, ed. J. A. Boydston, Vol. 2: 1902–1903, 271–92. Carbondale, IL: Southern Illinois University Press.

Dewey, J. 1978. *How we think*. In *John Dewey: The middle works, 1899–1924*, ed. J. A. Boydston, Vol. 6: 1910–1911, 177–356. Carbondale, IL: Southern Illinois University Press.

Dewey, J. 1980. *Democracy and education*. In *John Dewey: The middle works, 1899–1924*, ed. J. A. Boydston, Vol. 9: 1916, 1–402. Carbondale, IL: Southern Illinois University Press.

Dewey, J. 1984. *The quest for certainty: A study of the relation of knowledge and action*. In *John Dewey: The later works, 1925–1953*, ed. J. A. Boydston, Vol. 4: 1929, 1–250. Carbondale, IL: Southern Illinois University Press.

— ∽ —

Nineteen
Educator's Genuine Freedom

James G. Henderson

> *Genuine freedom, in short, is intellectual; it rests in the trained power of thought, in ability to 'turn things over,' to look at matters deliberately, to judge whether the amount and kind of evidence requisite for decision is at hand, and if not, to tell where and how to seek such evidence. If a man's actions are not guided by thoughtful conclusions, then they are guided by inconsiderate impulse, unbalanced appetite, caprice, or the circumstances of the moment. To cultivate unhindered, unreflective external activity is to foster enslavement, for it leaves the person at the mercy of appetite, sense, and circumstance.*
> —How We Think, MW 6: 232

I have a deep faith in educators' intellectual abilities. I think they are capable of engaging in sophisticated curriculum-based teaching inspired by a Socratic love of wisdom. This way of working can be characterized as a *deepening delibera-tion*, which I will explain shortly. I agree with Dewey that "genuine" freedom is tied to sophisticated deliberation; and Samuel Fleischacker (1999, 243) cogently summarized this point of view:

> *It may sound unexciting to announce that one wants to make the world free for good judgment, but this quiet doctrine turns out to be the most sensible, most decent, and at the same time richest concept of liberty we can possibly find. . . . A world where everyone can develop*

> *and use their own judgment as much as possible is closer to what we*
> *really want out of freedom.*

Consider the implications of this understanding of human freedom in educational work. Teachers would exercise their best professional judgment concerning their students' growth experiences in a way that would position students to gradually exercise responsible personal judgments concerning their own growth experiences. This is a generous and generative way of working. It is a wonderful vision of liberated teachers liberating students under their care. But can teachers work in this way? I firmly believe that the vast majority of teachers, if provided with the proper modeling and support, can meet this freedom-as-judgment challenge.

Freedom-as-Judgment

Freedom-as-judgment requires a curriculum-based instruction. Teachers who are "freeing" themselves by "freeing" their students must consider both the *hows* and *whys* of teaching. They cannot function as narrow technicians. They must cultivate the skills of their craft while thinking deeply about what they are doing. Pre-lesson, in-lesson, and post-lesson deliberations (or reflections) must be informed by a disciplined inquiry into the relationship between educational experience and human freedom. They must embrace a love of curriculum wisdom (Henderson and Kesson 2004).

Human *wisdom* is defined in the *Oxford English Dictionary* as "the capacity of judging rightly in matters relating to life and conduct; soundness of judgment in the choice of means and ends." Educators who adopt a wisdom orientation are challenging themselves to consider the "goodness" of their decisions. They are attempting to solve an immediate problem while cultivating enduring values. Their deliberations are situated in both the present and the visionary future.

John Dewey serves as a model for this professional commitment to a wisdom orientation. In a concise and insightful narrative on Dewey's philosophical work, Philip Jackson made two key points. First, Dewey considered replacing "experience" with "culture" as his key organizing term. Jackson (2002, 52–54) (author's emphasis) wrote:

> *Dewey's choice of the word* culture *to replace experience rested on what*
> *he had come to understand. . . . What Dewey found to be attractive about*
> *the notion of experience in the first place was its breadth of coverage. . . .*
> *[He was] openly committed to the goal of social betterment through the*
> *continued criticism of ongoing social practices and cultural traditions.*

Even after a long and productive scholarly career, Dewey still was studying and rethinking the relationship between educational experience and the "good" life. Second, there is no discernible method underlying Dewey's philosophical efforts. His inquiries are best understood as a way of living. Jackson (2002, 101) (author's emphasis) explained: "For Dewey . . . there was only the struggle *within experience* to . . . make life better for oneself and for others through an artful blend of thought, feeling, and action."

Reflective Inquiry

I believe that educators can work in this Deweyan spirit. Through the exercise of their own "artistry" of thought, feeling, and action, they can cultivate the emancipatory possibilities embedded in their students' educational experiences. To work in this way, they must develop certain *reflective inquiry* abilities. Over the years, I have attempted to conceptualize and provide guidance for this professional development work (Henderson and Hawthorne 2000; Henderson 2001); I briefly will summarize my latest effort here.

Curriculum and teaching deliberations can be conceptualized as a particular mode of inquiry. A mode of inquiry is a manner and mood of questioning and can be likened to a tone on a musical scale. As Dewey noted, the deliberative mode of inquiry is a turning over of possibilities. It is the examination and reexamination of how problems are defined and solved. It can be handled individually or collaboratively; if done with others, it usually involves negotiations.

Deepening Deliberation

A love of curriculum wisdom is practiced through a *deepening deliberation*—the infusion of six other modes of inquiry into the deliberative process. As I introduce these six inquiry modes, imagine a hologram in which each part of the picture contains the whole picture from a particular angle of vision. Each inquiry modality, though possessing unique features, is embedded in the other six modalities (Henderson and Kesson 2004):

- *Craft inquiry* is the continuous improvement of one's competence through thoughtful trial-and-error learning. It is the "tone" of technique and the "register" of best practice.
- *Poetic inquiry* is the soulful attunement to the creative process. It is the visionary, imaginative, and aesthetic mode celebrating personal meaning and expression.
- *Critical inquiry* is the examination of the political and economic subtexts of education. It is the articulation of righteous anger and resistance concerning matters of personal fairness and social justice, and it is utopian in its tone.
- *Dialogical inquiry* is the active seeking of diverse opinions. It is the embracing of self and others in the "logic" of reciprocal dialogue, and the recognition that the "truth" of some matter is situated in the play of perspectives.
- *Public moral inquiry* is the examination of the link between ethics and politics. Its concern is with congruence—with "walking the talk" of one's professional ideals.
- *Contemplative inquiry* is the exploration of the big picture of education in a society with democratic ideals. It has a prayerful, meditative tone.

I have faith in educators' abilities to work with all of these modes of curriculum inquiry. I recognize that this is a challenging form of professional artistry; but over years of research, I have been privileged to work with educators who resonate with this multimodal music!

I conclude with three insights I have acquired as I have attempted to advance curriculum-based teaching. First, a *deepening deliberation* is enacted in the small decision-making openings that exist in most teachers' workdays. Though the current educational policy environment is dominated by standards-based reform, with its command-and-control logic tied to high-stakes testing, there is generally some wiggle room to exercise professional judgment. Second, not all teachers are ready to build the necessary inquiry capacities, so this emancipatory effort must begin with educators who voluntarily function as collegial teacher leaders. Third, the enormous structural barriers to inquiry-based judgment must be confronted honestly and addressed through creative strategies.

Dewey (1972) had a deep faith in educators, as articulated in *My Pedagogical Creed.* I celebrate and share Dewey's faith as I contemplate teachers' genuine freedom.

References

Dewey, J. 1972. My pedagogic creed. In *John Dewey: The early works, 1882–1898,* ed. J. A. Boydston, Vol. 5: 1895–1898, 84–95. Carbondale, IL: Southern Illinois University Press.

Dewey, J. 1978. *How we think.* In *John Dewey: The middle works, 1899–1924,* ed. J. A. Boydston, Vol. 6: 1910–1911, 177–356. Carbondale, IL: Southern Illinois University Press.

Fleischacker, S. 1999. *A third concept of liberty: Judgment and freedom in Kant and Adam Smith.* Princeton, NJ: Princeton University Press.

Henderson, J. G. 2001, ed. *Reflective teaching: Professional artistry through inquiry,* 3rd ed. Upper Saddle River, NJ: Merrill/Prentice Hall.

Henderson, J. G., and R. D. Hawthorne. 2000. *Transformative curriculum leadership,* 2nd ed. Upper Saddle River, NJ: Pearson/Merrill/Prentice Hall.

Henderson, J. G., and K. R. Kesson. 2004. *Curriculum wisdom: Educational decisions in democratic societies.* Upper Saddle River, NJ: Merrill/Prentice Hall.

Jackson, P. W. 2002. *John Dewey and the philosopher's task.* New York: Teachers College Press.

— ∽ —

Twenty
A Spectator's Version of Knowledge

Deron Boyles

> *If we see that knowing is not the act of an outside spectator but of a participator inside the natural and social scene, then the true object of knowledge resides in the consequences of directed action.*
> —The Quest for Certainty: A Study of the Relation of Knowledge and Action, LW 4: 157

Armchair quarterbacks who complain about botched passes.

Well-meaning friends who suggest your child should play the violin.

Accountability-minded administrators who use checklists during classroom observations.

Each of these groups of people "knows" things. The armchair quarterback gets to see instant replays. The friend gets to project wishes onto a child he or she doesn't live with 24/7. The administrator gets to use a checklist to determine that a teacher needs better classroom management skills. Each group has knowledge. But the knowledge is not only limited, but also isn't that important. The armchair quarterback isn't actually on the field staring at an advancing defensive lineman and making immediate decisions about passing the football. The friend isn't around long enough to know whether the child is talented, disciplined, or even interested in music. The administrator isn't in the classroom with the various students long enough to understand the culture of a teacher's room.

Admittedly, teachers suffer from the same problem: they often treat their students as they are treated. Teachers become armchair quarterbacks, well-meaning friends, and administrators to their students. Covering material because of ITBS or other standardized testing constraints, assuming that they know what students need without first getting to know them, and imposing their own version of checklists in the form of worksheets and other busywork that are detached from students' lives—teachers fall into the same trap that Dewey warned us about.

We can't treat knowledge as a static entity. Knowledge isn't a series of discreet bits of information passed from a teacher to a student, even though that is a major assumption we carry with us. In fact, knowledge isn't really the point at all. *Knowing* is the point. And the risk in not understanding the difference is in turning students into the same kinds of spectators that armchair quarterbacks, well-meaning friends, accountability-minded administrators, and even teachers often represent.

The Relevance of the Spectator

Dewey's suggestion was twofold: (1) A statement about how things are may or may not correspond to how things actually are; (2) At the same time, it is not possible to treat this correspondence as if it were a matter of comparing the statement against reality. What we have to do is make judgments in "real time" about consequences of actions in solving actual problems. Correspondence, then, becomes a metaphor for Dewey, allowing him to argue that while a "spectator" version of knowledge is not always wrong, neither does it describe nor explain how people actually use information from their lives to solve their problems. The relevance of the "spectator" is in the very detachment Dewey rejected. "Spectators" don't assert; they passively observe. "Spectators" are outside of experience— at least the kind of experience that is engaging of others.

Knowing, Knowledge, and Intelligence

Distinguishing between a few key concepts may be helpful to better understand the larger meaning and its relationship to classroom interaction. Knowing, knowledge, and intelligence were distinct for Dewey. Knowing is a process of inquiry (involving specific instances of applied problem solving); knowledge constitutes the stable outcomes of inquiry; and intelligence is the result of the development and accumulation of capabilities to act (i.e., inquire) in specific ways.

Organic and natural environments for learning impel knowing and the habits of intelligence. Detachment from natural environments for learning indulges "spectating" and habits of routine. When you participate in the "consequences of directed action," you side with active inquiry. That is, given Dewey's theory of knowledge/knowing, classrooms should be places where students make knowledge claims at the same time they are engaged in knowing (inquiry). The means and ends were not separable for Dewey.

Active engagement of the sort Dewey suggested means that students engage rather than observe. They are not in the business of "discovering" the "facts" as though there is some cosmic puzzle to solve for once and for all. The point of inquiry is not to collect detached artifacts. Rather, active inquiry puts functionality above abstraction. Active inquiry means students identifying problems and actually solving them. As a result, a general pattern emerges when students use their own experiences (individual and joint) as a backdrop to solve other problems. Like an ever-expanding upward spiral, students develop and grow best when their interests are engaged and utilized.

Of course, not all inquiry is fruitful. That's why Dewey talked about "directed action." Some actions are whim and do not lead to educative experiences. Rather than "directing" students to be "spectators," the teacher directs students toward engaging activities—to active inquiry that leads to further inquiry (and knowing). Be clear: Directing students to prefabricated "learning centers" or "activity centers" to do busywork is not what Dewey was describing. Dewey advocated students becoming experimenters themselves.

The Quest for Certainty

Students, therefore, no longer search for "the truth" or "the right answers." Instead, students make assertions to be judged by the bounds of their own experiences—bounds that already exist and that expand via inquiry and directed action. This approach not only represents a big shift in our understanding of the roles of teachers and students, but also shifts the purpose of schooling away from "getting" answers, grades, diplomas, and jobs—which Dewey obliquely called the "quest for certainty."

Such a "quest for certainty" may be largely to blame for the general lack of inquiry found within U.S. classrooms. Students as testable objects themselves, and whose role it is to gather discreet bits of data and information, are largely subjected to a classroom sphere where the only evidence of relation is between imposed artifacts and superimposed goals. Even good teachers are burdened by the perversion of the "quest for certainty" seen in most schools. Never mind that the reality is itself subjectively constructed—all the tests, the standards, the mission statements, the learning objectives. The reality makes little difference, because the presentation of that reality is summed up as "the real world" or "the way it is." As a result, teacher-proof curricula, accountability policies, and the enormous focus on both standardization and competition arguably are examples of what Dewey would have considered misguided.

Of course, some teachers in some schools practice active inquiry, but they are few and far between. Preordained and prefabricated, the reality of most teacher and student roles in schools has been so long established that the task of changing the culture of schools is daunting. When education students begin their course work, they enter with ideas and experiences that inform what they want to do and how they want to do it. But these ideas are virtually unchanged from the culture from which they came. These students were reared as spectators (and often spectated in their college classes as well). Even when some education students profess to wanting to "engage" their students in "active" learning, the result usually is a souped-up version of traditional schooling.

Dewey's position, however, is an offering. It's a possible "out." It represents one way students and teachers might develop relations in less contrived ways than what currently goes on in most schools. By shifting roles of teachers and students so that both groups are inquirers into problems they face, the "quest for certainty" goes out the window and the expectations for both the "quest" and the "certainty" are challenged. In place of certainty is inquiry–*knowing*–and it comes into being when the engagement between teachers and students (and students and students, parents and students, etc.) supports investigations and experiments, leading to directed action and to continual knowing.

Reference

Dewey, J. 1984. *The quest for certainty: A study of the relation of knowledge and action.* In *John Dewey: The later works, 1925–1953,* ed. J. A. Boydston, Vol. 4: 1929, 1–250. Carbondale, IL: Southern Illinois University Press.

— ∽ —

Twenty-One
Transcending False Dichotomies: The Dynamics of Doubt and Certainty

Tom Kelly

> *Taken merely as doubt, an idea would paralyze inquiry. Taken merely as certainty, it would arrest inquiry. Taken as a doubtful possibility, it affords a standpoint, a platform, a method of inquiry.*
> —*How We Think*, MW 6: 265

Dewey posed this stiff challenge: How can teachers help their students steer a steady course between the Scylla of impulsive doubt and the Charybdis of absolute certainty? Put differently, Dewey suggested that in the context of a democratic society, at least two perspectives can undermine the ideal of thoughtful, fair-minded consideration of ideas, whether the ideas are familiar or novel, commonsensical or improbable.

On the one hand, habitual doubt about the merits of any idea may embody a relativistic view toward truth or goodness. This view (not necessarily held consciously) entails the twin notions that all ideas are as good or bad as any others and that no valid method exists for determining whether one idea is true or better than any other. As nothing can be proven by rational thought or argumentation, deliberation is essentially arbitrary, bluster, fruitless. Hedonism is as compelling as altruism. A modified Nike slogan rules: Just do your own thing.

The second problematic perspective presumes that ideas which deviate from what individuals believe to be absolutely true or good deserve to be summarily dismissed as essentially false or evil. Inquiry is unnecessary, misguiding, and subversive. Rather, fanatical intolerance of competing perspectives is dutiful for those passionate, courageous, and wise enough to embrace the Truth.

Doubtful Possibility

Fortunately, Dewey also hinted at a path toward minimizing these twin threats to sustaining civil discourse. Drawing on Dewey and others (Elbow 1986; Kelly 2004), several promising perspectives and strategies can be outlined. The first centers on Dewey's idea of "doubtful possibility . . . as a method of inquiry." With supportive insistence, teachers can facilitate their students' taking on alternating stances of methodological doubting and believing. Methodological doubting or skepticism, in one version, is widely embraced in school rhetoric and practice. As a brand of critical thinking, it is aimed at engaging students' minds in logical analysis with an eye toward recognizing formal flaws in reasoning (inconsistencies, contradictions, and faulty premises or assumptions).

Perhaps less popular in school practice, but nonetheless significant in purpose, is social-political critique, which encourages students to examine texts (e.g., commercial advertising, political campaign literature, and subject-matter textbooks) to uncover their biased manipulations and propaganda. The presumption is that dominant power seeks to perpetuate its own interest and will use available media to do so, with truth, justice, fairness, and inclusiveness continually at risk in the process. Thus, vigilant disciplined doubting of received "truths" represents a vital force to safeguard the very integrity of democracy.

Methodological Believing

As Dewey suggested, however, helping students perceptively question logical claims and social arrangements that might be marred, manipulated, or marginalizing is only half of what is needed to advance thoughtful, fair-minded inquiry. To counterbalance the standpoint of discriminating doubt, students need to develop the complementary capacity for methodological believing. Methodological believing can be likened to a game where the explicit purpose is to approach an idea provisionally from a generous, assenting, empathic viewpoint.

Students are encouraged not only to temporarily suspend their disbelief, but also more affirmatively and imaginatively to embrace the strong possibility that the idea is intriguing, helpful, and worthy of their efforts to deeply understand its meaning and favorable implications. Where confusion exists, an embrace of this provisional standpoint disciplines students to assume that the problem likely lies in their own insufficient understanding, not in the inadequacy of the idea. Hence, further inquiry—not dismissal—is activated. Directed to the author of the idea or to those appearing to understand it well, inquiry is activated along these lines:

- "Help me see what I might be overlooking or blocking. Help me experience the force of this perspective as you experience it."
- "If I were asked to dramatically portray this idea, I would want to deserve an Oscar nomination. Help me, while I'm temporarily playing this role, get to that level of appreciation."

Because of the alarm bells that misunderstanding of this method can generate, it is essential to emphasize that the intent of methodological believing is not to have students become obsequious, self-deprecating, indiscriminate adherents to any and all ideas. Just the opposite. The intent is to have students develop a deeper understanding and appreciation of the potential merits of all viewpoints as part of the process of deliberate, disciplined inquiry which, when coupled with methodological doubting, is designed to lead to more informed, fair-minded judgments of the overall worth of any idea.

Just as methodological believing corrects for the half empty and dismantling perspective of methodological doubting, methodological doubting, in turn, moderates the stance of affirmation and appreciation characteristic of methodological believing. Through the coupling of these methods, we experience Dewey's tendency to integrate apparent opposites in the process of exposing false either-or dichotomies. Witness in the quote cited how Dewey framed doubt and certainty not as oppositional forces, as they are characteristically understood, but as dynamics that possess common properties or propensities within the interpretative context of inquiry.

A significant implication for teachers follows from understanding Dewey's sustained critique of accepting false dichotomies. For Dewey, false dichotomies in general, and the excesses of doubt and certainty highlighted in the quote in particular, often function to choke curiosity, invalidate inquiry, incriminate interaction, intensify ignorance, and solidify stereotypes. They promote and perpetuate a preemptive polarization that tends to preclude complexity and overlook opportunities that can genuinely, not artificially, create connection and community.

To help students examine the dynamics of either-or and both-and perspective-taking, teachers might focus on these ideas: ambivalence, paradox and contradiction, and provocative declarations. Exploring ambivalence can provide students with a felicitously familiar context for understanding how clearly contrary emotions and directives—e.g., love and hate, holding on and letting go—often are experienced simultaneously, yet make utter psychological sense. In fact, with insightful exploration, these contrary emotions and directives emerge as intimately interdependent—that is, as precious paradoxes, not at all as contradictions. If apparent opposites can exist sensibly within us, maybe they can exist between us as well. Thus, distinguishing between contradictions and paradoxes in particular contexts seems to be a fruitful line of intellectual and social inquiry.

Provocative Declarations

Investigation can be enhanced through the use of provocative declarations. These are designed to invite students to dwell with increasing comfort and sophistication in the glorious, but challenging territory where the aesthetics are painted marvelous shades of gray, not black and white. Consider these samples:

- Being deliberate in judgment precludes being decisive.
- Vulnerability is a veritable weakness.
- To be female and critical is invariably to be or be seen as a shrew.
- To be attentive to seemingly dubious claims of irresponsible students is to be permissive.
- Conviction inevitably leads to close-mindedness.
- Love is a sweet torture.

Addressing controversy in the classroom demands from teachers a challenging inquiry artistry (for specifics, see Kelly 2004; and Henderson and Keeson 2004). When facilitated well, students confronting provocative declarations can experience a number of exemplary benefits. Among these benefits might be greater attentiveness to both the precision and malleability of language and the prevalence and preciousness of paradox; an appreciation for uncommon commonalities; fresh insight into taken-for-granted socialized "truths"; and a keener affirmation of this enterprise called inquiry.

I ask you, dear reader: How does this essay—and others—stand up to the disciplined use of methodological believing and doubting?

References

Dewey, J. 1978. *How we think.* In *John Dewey: The middle works, 1899–1924,* ed. J. A. Boydston, Vol. 6: 1910–1911, 177–356. Carbondale, IL: Southern Illinois University Press.

Elbow, P. 1986. *Embracing contraries: Explorations in learning and teaching.* New York: Oxford University Press.

Henderson, J. G., and K. R. Keeson. 2004. *Curriculum wisdom: Educational decisions in democratic societies.* Upper Saddle River, NJ: Pearson/Merrill Prentice Hall.

Kelly, T. 2004. A teacher educator's story. In *Curriculum wisdom: Educational decisions in democratic societies,* ed. J. G. Henderson and K. R. Keeson, 144–58. Upper Saddle River, NJ: Pearson/Merrill Prentice Hall.

— ∽ —

Twenty-Two
Turning Sunlight into Children

Marilyn Doerr

> *The distinction between wisdom and information is old, and yet requires constantly to be redrawn. Information is knowledge which is merely acquired and stored up; wisdom is knowledge operating in the direction of powers to the better living of life. Information, merely as information, implies no special training of intellectual capacity; wisdom is the finest fruit of that training. . . . [T]here is all the difference in the world whether the acquisition of information is treated as an end in itself, or is made an integral portion of the training of thought.*
> — How We Think, MW 6: 222

How *do* we think? Or, as my students sometimes say: "I *can't* think. I am too [tired, hungry, sick, bored, preoccupied] to make sense of it." They aren't sure *how* they do think, they just know what gets in the way of their being able to learn.

I am a high school science teacher. Science can be taught two ways: as a large group of data that has been accumulated and tweaked over many years, with vocabulary that needs to be memorized and equations that need to be practiced; or as a series of concepts that eventually cohere, where the learner begins to make connections between what is going on in his personal world and scientific research. The first way is an information process; the second way, a move toward wisdom.

Thinking Critically

Even the term "thinking" can be looked at as a definition to be memorized, a neuronal system to be learned, or a concept to be internalized. What exactly is physically going on in my body when I think and understand? What, for example, is the difference biologically between the mind and brain? When science is taught as a series of vocabulary words, the excitement, wonder, and curiosity of the discipline is lost or, worse, never tapped.

A teacher faces this dilemma every day of his or her teaching life, no matter what subject he or she teaches. How do I get my students to think and understand? To be more than just repositories of information that can be spit back for a quiz? Paulo Freire (1970) wrote about "banking information," where students are used merely as reservoirs in which to dump data. Memorization certainly has a role in learning, but it can never be the goal of learning. The goal of learning is critical thinking.

Acquiring Wisdom

No Child Left Behind, the mantra of the Bush administration, has brought memorization and multiple-choice testing to the forefront of public school education. Teachers are barraged with directives about how to prepare students for proficiency testing and how to raise scores. Little of those directives has anything to do with the acquisition of wisdom, of understanding. The emphasis is on the acquisition of information.

A fellow science educator, who mainly teaches AP Biology, was in a particularly deep funk one day. He had added a short essay question to a large test written by ETS (Educational Testing Service), the company that prepares and controls the AP program. To prepare for this test, his students had memorized the light and dark reactions of photosynthesis, the molecular structures of chlorophyll, glucose, and NADPH, and all the steps of the Krebs cycle. His short essay question was: What is the purpose of photosynthesis? Not one student in his classes answered the question correctly. They had garnered a great deal of information, but had no understanding of what they learned. They had built no constructs, created no relationships, seen no integration, developed no wisdom as to why photosynthesis may just be the most important process on our planet—or, as K. C. Cole (2003, 96) called it, "the alchemy that turns sunlight into children." This scenario is precisely what educators must guard against. It is no easy task.

Ranking the Concepts

One general rule I have created for myself, which may be helpful to others, is to think of a unit lesson in terms of concepts. When you decide on the main concepts you want to get across in a unit, rank those concepts. The concept you rank as #1 will guide everything you do in that unit. At the end, it will be the main question you will ask of your students. How they answer will help you decide whether or not the unit has been successful.

Consider an example. One class I teach, mainly to seniors, is Astronomy. A concept I work on endlessly is magnitude—the vast spaces in the universe and the sizes of bodies within those spaces. Little relative information exists on Earth that we can use to help explain the difference between the distance from New York to San Francisco—about 3,000 miles—and the distance between Earth and Alpha Centauri—27 trillion miles. And that is our second closest star!

If students learn about these vast distances only through a series of story problems in which they compute various distances, they will not understand them. They will not understand why we are not sure where the edge of the universe is, if there is an edge to the universe. They will not understand why finding other solar systems is so difficult. They will not understand that everything in the universe is moving away from everything else. They will not understand curved space, the Big Bang theory, or how galaxies are organized. These magnitudes have to become more than information. And so we construct manipulatives, use computers to view three-dimensional models, pace off distances in the classroom—anything we can think of to scaffold that concept of magnitude. The process often takes me nine months, and invariably I hear the same refrain from year to year: "This class gives me a headache."

It takes time to learn how to move from information to wisdom, from banked learning to understanding. Teachers must be patient with themselves. I have been teaching for many years, and I still have days when I am disappointed in myself. But educators must not be lulled into teaching only for information. A teacher's finest moments will come when giving that last-question essay on a test, and 90 percent of the students offer answers similar to the following:

> *I think the purpose of photosynthesis is to provide food for all living things—sometimes directly, like when the cow eats the grass, but more often indirectly, as when I eat the cow—and in that process taking the ongoing energy from the Sun and putting it into the tissues of every living being. Without photosynthesis, we have no way of getting all that energy. We are surrounded by it, but it is unavailable to us, kind of like being thirsty in a rowboat in the middle of the ocean.*

That is real pedagogy. That is real thinking. That is the beginning of wisdom.

References

Coles, K. C. 2003. *Mind over matter: Conversations with the cosmos.* Orlando, FL: Harcourt.

Dewey, J. 1978. *How we think.* In *John Dewey: The middle works, 1899–1924,* ed. J. A. Boydston, Vol. 6: 1910–1911, 177–356. Carbondale, IL: Southern Illinois University Press.

Freire, P. 1970. *Pedagogy of the oppressed,* trans. M. B. Ramos. New York: Continuum.

Twenty-Three
Reflecting on the Mentoring Relationship

Shelli L. Nafziger

> *Reflective thinking is always more or less troublesome because it involves overcoming the inertia that inclines one to accept suggestions at their face value; it involves willingness to endure a condition of mental unrest and disturbance. Reflective thinking, in short, means judgment suspended during further inquiry; and suspense is likely to be somewhat painful.*
> —*How We Think*, MW 6: 191

The act of reflection is the essence of a beautiful experience within the context of school. Particularly important in a mentoring relationship, reflection is distinctly viable if the mentor and mentee are aware of the logical steps of the process. These steps can be used as a guide with which a teacher-artist (the mentor) models and shares with the practicing teacher-artist (the mentee). The five steps of reflection, as delineated by Dewey (1978) are:

1. A felt difficulty
2. Its location and definition
3. Suggestion of possible solution
4. Development by reasoning of the bearings of the suggestion
5. Further observation and experiment leading to its acceptance or rejection; that is, the conclusion of belief or disbelief

Step 1: A Felt Difficulty

Felt difficulty generally arises out of a shared educational experience between a practicing teacher-artist and a teacher-artist. The power of suggestion causes the participants in the relationship to be uneasy, maybe even uncomfortable with the experience. This feeling of discomfort is frustrating, yet important for both members of the mentoring relationship. For the Step 1 process to be healthy, the mentor has to appreciate the mentee's felt difficulty. Though challenging, the mentor must allow a mentee to experience this feeling without jumping in to save the situation.

This felt difficulty is critical, if not essential, for reflection to be successful and for thinking to be prosperous. As Dewey (1978, 189) suggested, "Thinking begins in what fairly enough may be called a forked-road situation, a situation which is ambiguous, which presents a dilemma, which proposes alternatives." This tug-of-war experienced by individuals in the relationship should be exposed carefully and communicated as a logical first step of reflection. If this felt difficulty is not experienced, there will not be a need for reflection. Dewey (1978,

189) explained, "As long as our activity glides smoothly along from one thing to another, or as long as we permit our imagination to entertain fancies at pleasure, there is no call for reflection."

Step 2: Its Location and Definition

A critical second step is essentially located in the context of a given situation upon which a mentor and mentee pass judgment or allow conclusions to enter into the experience. In the context of a problem situation, the mentee must, with the help of the mentor, "suspend judgment"; or, in the case of Step 2, remove the location or definition of a situation to truly understand the nature of the problem (Dewey 1978, 238).

Dewey suggested, in fact, that someone outside the field of teaching should mentor the reflective process of a mentee. He (1984, 16) stated, "Ordinary phenomena are reflected upon in detachment from the conditions and rises under which they exhibit themselves in practice." For Step 2 of the process of reflection, this position is significant, especially in the age of accreditation and assessment. For example, a practicing teacher-artist gets assessed on his or her abilities to perform teaching acts. The felt difficulty within the evaluation process of the apprenticeship is having the mentor serve two functions: one as a mentor/coach and the other as an evaluator of the process. Perhaps Dewey is suggesting that the mentor, to be truly effective in this stage of reflection, needs to be removed from the evaluation process in the context of a shared experience.

Step 3: Suggestion of Possible Solution

Critically, for an analysis or judgment to be on target, the mentor must guide the practicing teacher-artist through the suggestion of a possible solution. The mentor logically helps guide the mentee as they study the context and determine a possible solution to a given situation. Without a mentor, many suggestions could justifiably be unclear, misplaced, undefined, or inappropriate. The information gathered by the mentee in Step 2 could be misinterpreted because of a lack of contextual experience. Communication must be clear regarding a suggested solution.

Step 4: Development by Reasoning of the Bearings of the Suggestion

The process of understanding the implications of any solution to any problem is termed *reasoning*. Step 4 evolves from Step 3 as the mentor and mentee consider the implications of the suggested solutions on which they have reflected. The mentor and mentee, through the power of language, discover underlying possibilities by digging deeper into a situation and ultimately suspending initial disbelief. In short, they explore all options.

The mentor and mentee reflect on suggestions and exchange views. The essence of Step 4 occurs when the suggested ideas are studied for implications.

That is, the practicing teacher-artist uncovers ideas about a situation and then analyzes the implications of each of those ideas.

The question remains: How does the context of the situation change or remain the same? To comprehend Steps 3 and 4, imagine a classroom in which the children are actively working on a social studies art project. The classroom is busy; children are cutting, gluing, coloring, and folding. As an observer, the practicing teacher-artist assumes that the art project is going smoothly.

Dewey would suggest that we suspend initial judgment and dig deeper for underlying suggestions that may demonstrate an opposing argument. Shortly after the initial inference, a child approaches the practicing teacher-artist with his art replica of an Egyptian pyramid. The practicing teacher-artist is amazed and dismayed. In contrast to her expectations, the corners of the pyramid are not mathematically at right angles, the base of the pyramid is too small, and the faces of the pyramid are all different sizes. What a mess!

The power of suggestion and possible inferred analysis by the practicing teacher-artist is that the child did not listen to the directions. How could he, by such a wide margin, have missed the point of the project? Again, the practicing teacher-artist scans the classroom and breathes a sigh of relief because most of the children are on task and appear to have understood the concept. At this point, the practicing teacher-artist, with the aid of the mentor, through rich language, develops ideas about the young boy based on suggestions and inferences embedded in the experience. They define the problem vis-à-vis Step 2. The rich experiences of the mentor prove invaluable.

Step 3 invites possible suggestions. Is the child a slow learner? Does he have a hearing problem? Was he fidgeting or daydreaming when the practicing teacher-artist modeled the project? Does he dislike art projects? Was he being difficult and seeking negative attention from the teacher? All these questions lend themselves to possible ideas and implications about the boy's problem.

With the process of deduction, an individual begins with all the possibilities of a given situation and, through the process of inferring, suggesting, uncovering, and implying, deduces the suggested whole and arrives at an idea. About deduction, Dewey (1978, 256) stated, "The final test of deduction lies in the experimental observation. Elaboration by reasoning may make a suggested idea very rich and very plausible, but will not settle the validity of that idea." Herein lies the rationale for Step 5.

Step 5: Further Observation and Experiment Leading to Its Acceptance or Rejection; That Is, the Conclusion of Belief or Disbelief

At Step 4, Dewey (1978, 242) argued that the "conclusion is hypothetical or conditional." He (1978, 240) suggested that, through Step 5, we must be involved with some kind of "experimental corroboration, or verification, of the conjectural idea." Dewey relayed the importance of testing a hypothesis, much like a scientist does when conducting an experiment.

In recent years, the term *action research* has risen to the forefront of teacher classroom inquiry. In some components of action research, the teacher observes, researches, and questions an idea. The teacher-researcher then tests a hypothesis within the context of an educational situation. The results follow, allowing the teacher and others to benefit. Perhaps Dewey was asking for a similar methodology in Step 5. The practicing teacher-artist must test the inferred ideas and their implications. If the results agree, a conclusion is confirmed.

Building on the previous example, the practicing teacher questioned why the boy had difficulty with the art project. Based on Dewey's steps of reflection, she concluded that she must test her ideas as to why the boy had difficulty with the project. Each idea is tested using the same context and conditions defined previously, and her results are very different from her initial hypothesis. He was not being difficult by seeking negative attention; in fact, he needed glasses.

Thank goodness, the young boy can now see; and so can his teacher. In Step 5, a suggested solution is either confirmed or denied; if it is confirmed, it is helpful for the future. So this last step of reflection takes us into the future.

References

Dewey, J. 1978. *How we think.* In *John Dewey: The middle works, 1899–1924,* ed. J. A. Boydston, Vol. 6: 1910–1911, 177–356. Carbondale, IL: Southern Illinois University Press.

Dewey, J. 1984. *The sources of a science of education.* In *John Dewey: The later works, 1925–1953,* ed. J. A. Boydston, Vol. 5: 1929–1930, 1–40. Carbondale, IL: Southern Illinois University Press.

— ∽ —

Twenty-Four
Making Informed Judgments

Dan Marshall

> *The essence of critical thinking is suspended judgment.*
> —How We Think, MW 6: 238

Shortly after introducing an activity in class, I observed a more or less typical display of apparent student engagement, ranging from raised-voice discussion accompanied by waving arms and pointing fingers, to fluttering-eyed, head-dropping somnambulism. After scanning the room for several minutes from a fixed location, I began to wander, having decided that some of the students could use my help. Roaming the room, using physical proximity along with some calculated questions and comments to "encourage" select students to join in, I felt satisfied that all was well.

Teachers are, by definition, consummate judges and decision makers. This is, in large part, because our work is action-oriented and student-related. Day after day, we find ourselves identifying situations, weighing options, making choices, and taking actions. However, this routine creates its own problems. As Maxine Greene (1988, 4) noted:

> *It is clear that choice and action both occur within and by means of ongoing transactions with objective conditions and with other human beings. They occur as well within the matrix of a culture, its prejudgments, and its symbol systems.*

The Problem with Routine

This ever-present decision-making problematic for teachers has much to do with the judgmental aspect of our choices. Briefly, all decisions are choices typically made on the basis of habit or custom (it's the way we do things), external force or influence (it's the way the district or state wants things done), or deliberate (i.e., intelligent) choice among alternatives (it's what ought to happen, given the evidence).

In the worst cases, decisions can reflect little or no deliberate judgment at all; that is, we make them reflexively, without sufficient knowledge or careful comparison of our options. In the best cases, teachers recognize the inherent traps within what Greene (1988) called our cultural matrix, particularly its established prejudgments (e.g., some students are lazy), as well as the apparent external forces that impinge upon our choices (e.g., high-stakes testing pressures), and then, skeptical of the preceding, set out to gather whatever information is necessary for us to select the best option. The resulting decision is said to reflect an *informed judgment*.

Informed Judgment

Later, when I had some time to reflect, I found myself cataloging the names of students I had "visited" during the activity. One student seemed frequently disengaged with class as a whole, while a second often had difficulty keeping social chat separate from activity-based talk. One student probably hadn't done the requisite reading, while another may have felt inferior within his small group and tuned out as a protective measure.

Judgment involves the consideration of different options before arriving at a decision regarding their comparative merit or worth. To judge, therefore, is to form a value-oriented opinion or understanding—to find the *best* choice available. Decisions resulting from *informed judgments* represent the combination of efforts to bring our intellect (i.e., deliberation) into play with our value-grounded understandings and dispositions when choosing among different options. In contrast, many—perhaps most of our teaching decisions—are made "on the fly" and without the benefit of much informed judgment. Teachers' work is hectic, reflecting a kind of routine immediacy unlike almost any other professional work. Taking the time to consider the circumstances, the voracity of available information, and the options at hand seems impossible when we don't have the time in the first place.

Consequently, the intelligent or deliberative basis for judgment prior to our decision making often goes unattended. This happens too because we often seem to find ourselves making familiar, routine, almost habitual decisions based on our teaching situations and contexts. In my case, I looked around the room, determined that some students had decided to ignore their responsibilities, and chose to provide them with a little extrinsic motivation.

Prejudgment

The embarrassing part, for me, is that on reflection, my judgment, my action, and my subsequent reflection on both were merely habitual. I was not acting intelligently, nor later that day was I thinking intelligently. Mine were *prejudgments* stemming from my teaching cultures. I was not thinking much, and I certainly was not thinking critically about the situation before me. To do so, I would have had to suspend my judgment—to have looked over the room and decided *not* to make a decision about what I was seeing at that moment. For Dewey, suspended judgment is the essence of critical thinking.

Several days later, I was led to reflect on this same activity and, more importantly, my judgments about it and the students in class. What led me to this revisiting is another story entirely, but what I learned about myself remains deeply troubling.

In his dictionary of Dewey's thoughts, Ralph Winn (1959, 18) reminded us that Dewey understood criticism as "discriminating judgment" and "careful appraisal" regarding value-laden choices. What makes serious thinking *critical* is the ability to bring "the possible" or "the ideal" to bear on what we take to be the situation at hand (Winn 1959, 138). That is, we carefully appraise the situation and imagine it, if only for a moment, as it could or should be in an ideal sense.

Suspended Judgment

Had I suspended my judgment momentarily, I might have doubted my matter-of-fact thinking processes. My take on the class activity had everything to do with off-task behavior and how to fix that problem. Thinking more critically, I might have wondered about the nature of the task itself (a single task with little individual flexibility), or my narrow-minded notion of on-task behavior (not to mention my ignoring of the purposes of the activity), or my choice to "police the area" rather than engage certain students in conversation about their impressions of the activity.

Ironically, I try my best to help undergraduate and graduate students value and develop what I call a "healthy skepticism" about their pedagogical decisions; for what we think we know, or feel, or can do underlies not only our judgments but our choices and actions as teachers. I routinely encourage them to base their pedagogical decisions on informed judgment, as Henderson and Kesson (2004, 45) reminded us: "If educators do not take on the responsibility of making informed judgments directed by intelligence, the profession will increasingly find itself subject to the decisions of others." This is, I tell them, not an easy responsibility. Even after teaching for more than 25 years, I continue to struggle with it.

References

Dewey, J. 1978. *How we think*. In *John Dewey: The middle works, 1899–1924*, ed. J. A. Boydston, Vol. 6: 1910–1911, 177–356. Carbondale, IL: Southern Illinois University Press.

Greene, M. 1988. *The dialectic of freedom*. New York: Teachers College Press.

Henderson, J. G., and K. R. Kesson. 2004. *Curriculum wisdom: Educational decisions in democratic societies*. Upper Saddle River, NJ: Pearson/Merrill/Prentice Hall.

Winn, R. B., ed. 1959. *John Dewey: Dictionary of education*. New York: Philosophical Library.

— ∽ —

Twenty-Five
Unexamined Presumptions

George W. Noblit

> *Prejudice is the acme of the* a priori. *Of the* a priori *in this sense we may say what is always to be said of habits and institutions: They are good servants, but harsh and futile masters.*
> —Experience and Objective Idealism, MW 3: 136

Our view of people and things different from us has little to do with them per se. It springs not from our direct experience with others but from beliefs that exist beneath our consciousness—presumptions that we have not examined and that are not always evident to us. From these unexamined presumptions emerge prejudgments of experiences. These exist before experience and stop us from learning fully from our experience.

The bind of *a priori* beliefs is strong and many people never see beyond them, accepting them as natural and therefore correct. As Dewey noted, the *a priori* left to their own master us, making us pawns of our culture and society. However, the *a priori* examined is the tool, the servant, of learning from our experiences—for seeing the opposite gender, people of other races, the poor, and so on, anew—to see them from our experiences, not from our biases. Such experiences are truly educative, and I believe understanding them is necessary to be able to teach well.

Commitment to Equity

As an educator, I long ago decided to devote my work and life to equity. I came of age in the 1960s when it seemed we were clearer about the inequities in our society and more committed to broad-based social action to reduce, even eliminate, inequity. I did not come to a commitment to equity easily. I grew up in a small industrial mountain community full of the prejudices of class, ethnic heritage (against Southern and Eastern Europeans), gender, and race. I inherited these as natural facts of life. I also perpetuated these in many ways as I defined myself superior based on my maleness and whiteness.

Probably through the lens of class and ethnicity, I first saw the unfairness of prejudices. To be honest, however, I was more attuned to the unfairness of class hierarchies because they directly affected me. Because I was working class, I was unable to date some girls and hang out with some boys. I was unable to see much further than myself at that time. In retrospect, I had little consciousness of my role in creating inequities nor did I have a language to enable me to talk about inequity beyond my own self-absorption.

Consciousness Raising

Later in my life, my consciousness was "raised," to use the language of the 1960s. In a world rocked by civil disobedience, all my prejudices were assaulted. The civil rights movement, women's movement, anti-war movement, and the youth movement gave way to race riots, marches, and political and personal confrontations. I recall being both scared and exhilarated. I was seeing the world and myself anew, and I was learning from my experiences in ways no book could teach.

Learning from these experiences changed my perspective on the world and thus confirmed for me Dewey's observation that prejudice emerges from the *a priori*. However, the immediacy of my experiences and the severity of the challenges to the boy I had been meant that the changes I focused on were internal.

Later, as a professor, I came to embrace the *a priori* in a new way. Up to that point, I was recounting my changes and my new beliefs as testimony to what others could, and should, believe. This, however, was not much of a pedagogy. As I struggled to find a way to teach against racism and sexism, I rediscovered the *a priori* not as an enemy but, as Dewey noted, as a servant of learning. My goal then became to be less a proselytizer of my way of understanding and more a teacher. I began to structure lessons ("gigs" I have come to call them for their performative, improvisational nature) that would reveal *a priori* beliefs and demonstrate how these beliefs were not only unfair to others but also reduced the possibilities that could be conceived of by the person with the *a priori* beliefs.

One of my favorite type of gigs requires students to face the hidden curriculum of a writing assignment. I ask them to analyze how my assigning them a paper that I will grade is reproductive of the social order and how one might create from the assignment an emancipating experience. The important element of this gig is that the paper has no assigned content—just that they are to write a paper and I will grade it. My students tell me that they alternatively love and hate the assignment, and me, as they work through it. The assignment comes at a point where we have read and discussed a set of ideas about structure and agency, how societies reproduce themselves, and how knowledge and reality are social constructions.

The result is almost always that students discover they have a language for expressing their ideas—one that I did not have in my youth or young adult years. Moreover, if one of us does not find the language—then we all go back and work through the material again. For me, seeing the *a priori* and struggling with it must be a collective accomplishment. If it is not, then the *a priori* is left a "harsh and futile master" for some, and students are left to believe that learning from experience is limited to personal awareness—but not a tool for educative development of our society.

As a teacher, I know that I still have much to learn. Yet this quotation from Dewey largely encapsulates what I have learned so far and also what I see as the most important substance I can teach.

Reference

Dewey, J. 1977. Experience and objective idealism. In *John Dewey: The middle works, 1899–1924*, ed. J. A. Boydston, Vol. 3: 1903–1906, 128–44. Carbondale, IL: Southern Illinois University Press.

— ∞ —

PART IV
INQUIRY AND EDUCATION

Inquiry and Education:
A Way of Seeing the World

Donna Adair Breault

What is inquiry? Dewey has a great deal to say regarding this question. Throughout his writings, he made numerous references to, and offered many characterizations of, inquiry. In *A Common Faith* (1986, 18), he called it "an unseen power . . . of the ideal." In *How We Think* (1978, 245), he spoke of the inquiry process as one in which we enter a contract as thinkers, as something that culminates and is ultimately weaved into a "coherent fabric." In that same book, Dewey (1978, 290) talked about the need to be playful when it comes to inquiring so that we can achieve a "largeness and imaginativeness of vision." In *The Quest for Certainty* (1984), Dewey helped us to understand that through the inquiry process, knowledge becomes a verb, something active and used for some purpose, by comparing it to the work a tool does rather than the tool itself.

Dewey also spent a great deal of time and attention letting us know what inquiry is *not*. In *The Quest for Certainty* (1984, 222), he warned that inquiry should be "the last thing to be picked up casually and clung to rigidly." Again and again, he argued that inquiry is not stagnant. It involves an active and purposeful process. In *How We Think* (1978, 264), for example, he cautioned us that thinking is not just a matter of storing past memories as if in some "antiseptic refrigerator," but involves using our past experiences and understandings for a purpose. Similarly, in *Democracy and Education* (1980), he admonished that we should not fill our heads like a scrapbook with facts that do not lead to solving real problems.

Not Spectators

In essence, we are not spectators. Learning involves active and purposeful engagement. This is a very different view of knowledge than more traditional views. It means that we are part of the meaning-making process. We cannot separate ourselves from what is known. Knowledge is not a bunch of "stuff" out there to be acquired, transmitted, and maintained. Instead, knowledge is a verb. It is an active and continually evolving process. Inquiry, according to Dewey, encapsulates that process of coming to know. With this image in mind, it is important to explore why it is important to promote inquiry within the classroom. I offer three such reasons.

First, if you make inquiry a focus of your work as a teacher, you become empowered. You have a voice in what happens in your classroom. This is not to say that you can ignore the curriculum and policy mandates that are part of your system, but it does mean that you can filter those mandates through a belief system and determine the best means through which you act as a teacher. Now more than ever, with No Child Left Behind creating such dreadful circumstances in our schools, you need to empower yourself through inquiry.

Think about it. You make more decisions as a teacher than almost any other person in any other profession. On what do you base those decisions? Tradition? Do you do something because it's what your teachers did when you were in school? Do you do something because it's what you saw your supervising teacher do when you were student teaching? Do you do something because you were taught to do it that way through a prescriptive in-service? Maybe it's just the way you've always done it, and if it isn't broken, why change it? Do you make choices based on convenience? Is it the easiest way to do something? Does it take less time to do it that way? Do you do something for lack of alternatives? Maybe you don't know any other way to do it. If you make inquiry a priority in your professional life, you do something because you believe it to be the best practice based on your beliefs and your understanding of teaching and learning. That is what makes you a professional. That is what keeps you excited about your job.

Second, if you make inquiry a priority in your classroom, you will empower others— namely, your students. Imagine that you have on a pair of sunglasses. While wearing those glasses, you see things around you differently. Likewise, to inquire is to see the world differently. Inquiry is not an external skill that can be trained, imitated, or prescribed; it is an inherent capacity each person possesses. You may have to learn how to use it, how to recognize it, the need to value it, the permission to explore it—but it is there. The degree to which you engage in inquiry will significantly impact your life as a teacher, and the degree to which you promote it in your classroom will significantly impact the lives of your students. I believe that the manner in which our world is changing makes it absolutely necessary for our students to think critically, and that won't happen unless teachers can think critically. Inquiry has to become a culture within each classroom. It has to be a way of seeing the world.

Finally, we must make inquiry the focus of our work in education because it is the sole means through which we will achieve reform in schools. Think of all the reform efforts that have failed over the years. Like the pendulum swinging metaphor, most reforms fail because they are imposed in a prescriptive manner, followed half-heartedly—and dismissed too readily. As long as we continue to blindly follow prescriptive efforts, nothing in education will change. Cuban (1993) looked at 7,000 profiles of classrooms from previous studies and observations spanning 1890 to 1990. In his study, Cuban noted few changes in the way teachers taught. Most of the instruction was teacher-centered. Passive learning—teacher-centered learning—will continue to dominate classrooms where reflection or inquiry is not the professional focus of the teacher. Until we make a lifelong commitment to inquiry, things will not change.

Images of Inquiry

Think again about the sunglasses. Let them represent your ability to inquire. Some of you will be comfortable wearing these glasses and probably will keep them on most, if not all, of the time. For some, wearing them may not be natural and may be difficult. You may start out wearing them for only small amounts of time and for only specific situations. As you mature as a professional, you may find yourself able to wear them more and more. Also consider the tint of the glasses. It will be different for everyone. For some, the tint may be a bit rosy. For others, it will be darker—particularly those who find themselves wrestling with issues of power and justice.

Have you ever had your eyes examined by a doctor and endured one of those large machines they put in front of your face? Think about that process. The eye doctor makes slight changes in the lens strengths and then asks, "Is it better this way or that?" The process is what you will do as a reflective practitioner. You will play around with images of inquiry to determine which "fits" and allows you to see things more clearly. To this end, the editors of this volume hope that the images of inquiry offered by the contributors in this section help you to refine your own image and help you to see its place within your work.

References

Cuban, L. 1993. *How teachers taught: Constancy and change in American classrooms, 1890–1990*, 2nd ed. New York: Teachers College Press.

Dewey, J. 1978. *How we think*. In *John Dewey: The middle works, 1899–1924*, ed. J. A. Boydston, Vol. 6: 1910–1911, 177–356. Carbondale, IL: Southern Illinois University Press.

Dewey, J. 1980. *Democracy and education*. In *John Dewey: The middle works, 1899–1924*, ed. J. A. Boydston, Vol. 9: 1916, 1–402. Carbondale, IL: Southern Illinois University Press.

Dewey, J. 1984. *The quest for certainty: A study of the relation of knowledge and action*. In *John Dewey: The later works, 1925–1953*, ed. J. A. Boydston, Vol. 4: 1929, 1–250. Carbondale, IL: Southern Illinois University Press.

Dewey, J. 1986. *A common faith*. In *John Dewey: The later works, 1925–1953*, ed. J. A. Boydston, Vol. 9: 1933–1934, 1–60. Carbondale, IL: Southern Illinois University Press.

— ∽ —

Twenty-Six
The Power of an Ideal

Jim Garrison

> *An unseen power controlling our destiny becomes the power of an ideal. . . . The artist, scientist, citizen, parent, as far as they are actuated by the spirit of their callings, are controlled by the unseen. For all endeavor for the better is moved by faith in what is possible, not by adherence to the actual.*
> —*A Common Faith*, LW 9: 17

Many teachers experience their choice to enter teaching in the etymological sense of "vocation" that derives from *vocare*, a calling. If you are among those who entered teaching because you experienced a call to serve, perhaps you felt possessed by something unseen, difficult to name, and beyond your capacity to control or even fully comprehend. The word "religion" derives from a root that means being bound or tied to a particular way of life. At the start of your career, you felt bound to your calling, to the particular way of life that is teaching. Do you still?

The Spirituality of Teaching

Whether committed to formal religion or not, you may have a sense of religious wonder, a natural piety toward the infinite plenitude of existence and your place in it. This attitude is born of passion, guided by imagination, and sustained by intelligent faith in possibility. It is a source of wisdom lying beyond knowledge of ideas and facts alone. That is why even those who have taught for many years without losing the call often still find it difficult to articulate their spiritual sense of teaching.

We may think of spirituality as an intimate, dynamic, and harmonious union with the universe that sustains us, wherein our creative acts matter. Dewey thought every individual an active participant in an unfinished and unfinishable universe rather than a spectator of a complete or completable creation. Our senses do not engender universal unity and harmony unaided. Such unity is not a fact of existence; indeed, there is a great deal of evidence to the contrary. This unity lies beyond the actual state of affairs in our world as we find it today, or in any other day, in the history of humankind. Unity is an unseen ideal, discerned only by emotion and imagination, of a possible cosmos beyond the chaos of our actual everyday affairs. For those who feel called and whose faith sustains them, imaginary ideals take possession of them with a power they cannot resist. For those with courage to believe and the passion to pursue things unseen, along with the honesty to accept what their intelligently guided inquiry discloses, the age of revelation is not past. Initially, such a powerful spiritual ideal seems far beyond the call to teach, but it is not.

The death of a single living creature is a greater loss to the universe than the collapse of a whole galaxy lacking living beings. And the procreation of a child is a grander act of creation than the constitution of lifeless worlds. When teachers connect and care for such divine beings and help awaken in them the light of learning, they bring into existence a radiance that outshines the brightest sun. Such care and creation has wonderful spiritual qualities.

Caring and Creativity

Teachers enter teaching and remain for two principal reasons. First, they seek to care for their students, connect with them, and help them learn and grow. Some are not even afraid to say they love their students. Second, they seek creative autonomy. Nothing known to us is more precious than intimate relations with other human beings, nor anything more miraculous than contributing to creating a life worth living for others and ourselves. Therein reside the spiritual values of the call to teach even when it remains hidden beneath the daily details of busy classroom lives. This spirituality gives the most profound meaning to the simplest acts of teaching. Immaculate moments are always waiting to shine through the clouds.

The busyness demanded by the bureaucratic forces of unreflective accountability does much to extinguish creativity and connection in teaching and thereby cancels the spiritual values that call and sustain teachers. Instead of honoring the numinous, technocrats reduce everything to numbers. They do not see students and teachers as unique human beings that must achieve a unique destiny to make unique contributions to a free and democratic community. Instead, they reduce students and teachers to calculable ciphers in the economic production function.

The powers which control our destiny demand that we adhere to the actual conditions of material existence rather than demonstrate faith in unseen possibilities. Confronted with such conditions, many teachers burn out and leave. Only those of you who have the imagination to comprehend the possible beyond the actual, the faith in things unseen, and who answer your calling wisely will find the values and courage you need to sustain yourself. You are among those teachers who abide in the place to which you were called while finding intimate, harmonious, and creative union with the larger whole of which you are a part. You are among those who realize the meaningful ideals of the spirit instead of the materialistic ideals of mammon.

Reference

Dewey, J. 1986. *A common faith*. In *John Dewey: The later works, 1925–1953*, ed. J. A. Boydston, Vol. 9: 1933–1934, 1–60. Carbondale, IL: Southern Illinois University Press.

— ∽ —

Twenty-Seven
Imagination of Ideal Ends

Craig A. Cunningham

> *Imagination of ideal ends pertinent to actual conditions represents the fruition of a disciplined mind.*
> —*A Common Faith*, LW 9: 35

In *A Common Faith*, Dewey described his naturalized conception of God as the active union, or unification, of the actual and the ideal. While such a union has its mystical or spiritual aspects, for Dewey the most ubiquitous and consequently interesting instances of the union of the actual and the ideal occur in everyday situations involving the application of intelligence to solving practical problems. Such an application of intelligence is, for Dewey, the ultimate expression of the human mind.

Dewey's project in *A Common Faith* was to develop a conception of God that could transcend the specific differences of religions or sects and show that religious experience is a universal element of all human experiences. Religions tend to emphasize what distinguishes them from other religions, resulting in further divisions and separations in an already-divided humanity. Dewey believed that an understanding of the *common* aspects of all religious experiences could help overcome these separations. While his project ultimately failed—because the particularities of each religious tradition cannot simply be ignored by the followers of that tradition, and because Dewey's reconstruction missed key aspects of what many consider to be the most essential aspects of religion—the book has value as a guide to the ways that ideals and actual conditions interact in myriad situations.

Desirable Ends

Every uncertain situation in life, Dewey suggested, contains a wide range of possible outcomes or endings. (Dewey called these simply "ends.") Some of these outcomes are desirable while others are not. Desirable ends are those that fulfill the needs or wants of the people involved. The most desirable ends are those that fulfill more needs or more wants for more people. An *ideal end* is that outcome which resolves a situation such that all possible good is realized while any possible negative consequences are avoided. Once an ideal end is chosen, the ideal can be used as a tool for guiding decision making toward the goal of realizing that end. Thus, ideals are tools for solving problems.

The process of selecting a particular end as *ideal* is a process of inquiry or deliberation, in which various possible solutions to a problem or uncertainty are considered. Each possible outcome is examined to determine both how it could be realized and what would be the results if it ensues. Remember that these outcomes don't *exist* initially in any concrete sense. Rather, they are present only in the *imagination*. But imagination should not be dismissed as mere flights of fancy or escape from reality. Rather, imagination is a means for solving problems, especially if it pays attention to real or actual conditions while envisioning ends that are really possible or desirable.

Pertinence

Dewey provided a single word that gives us a clue to the relation of ideal ends to actual conditions: "pertinent." What is it that makes an ideal end *pertinent* to actual conditions? The word does not imply a direct causal link between the ideal ends and the conditions. Pertinence is not a straightforward criterion that can be turned into a formula and simply applied in multiple situations. The *Shorter Oxford English Dictionary* defines *pertinent* as: "Appropriate, suitable in nature or character; relating to the matter in hand, relevant; to the point; apposite." The words "suitable" and "appropriate" seem to be key synonyms.

How does a person know whether a possible outcome, or end, is "pertinent" to actual conditions? Dewey told us that it takes a "disciplined mind" to imagine ends that are pertinent to actual conditions. This phrase has two related meanings. A "disciplined" mind is one that has been trained to think effectively, presumably through practice in thinking in a wide variety of situations. But "disciplined" also implies that a mind has acquired the concepts and techniques of one or more disciplines in the academic sense: science, history, art, or mathematics. A "disciplined" mind is better able to imagine suitable or appropriate ideal ends because a disciplined mind is better able to think clearly and to apply a wide range of knowledge and concepts in new situations. A disciplined mind doesn't waste time with impossible or undesirable outcomes, but focuses on those ends that are both possible and desirable. A disciplined mind, in other words, is one that uses imagination effectively and efficiently in the choice of suitable solutions to problems.

A simple hypothetical example might help to clarify this process. Suppose that you are driving down the highway at night, in winter, and you get a flat tire. Immediately you are plunged into an uncertain situation. Should you keep driving on the flat tire and hope that you reach a gas station before you destroy the wheel of your car? Should you get out your jack and install the spare? Or should you use your cell phone to call for help? Someone who lacks a disciplined mind may simply panic and fail to consider actual conditions. A more mature or disciplined person will be able to set aside the emotions of fear and panic and focus on reality.

Suppose for a moment that you do not have a cell phone, but you have a spare and a jack in the trunk. However, when you try to loosen the lug nuts on the flat, you discover that the lug nuts will not move. This is certainly a "pertinent" condition! A person who understands physics may know that more leverage can be applied with a longer lug wrench. Or, you may realize that the lug nuts may be rusted in place and that you need a spray lubricant to loosen the nuts. Or, the problem may be that the lug wrench is missing, and the situation involves a choice between trying to flag down passersby or trying to drive to a gas station. Each option presents various difficulties. A knowledge of the geographical area may help you to know whether it is safe to stand outside the car waving your arms.

Imagination

The importance of this idea for teachers is the strong connection it makes between disciplining the mind—teaching it to think and to know—and the imagination. Rather than seeing imagination as the opposite of thought, Dewey suggested that imagination is a key aspect of creative and successful thinking.

Teachers themselves are problem solvers, often working in uncertain situations with multiple goals. In any given situation, what is the best possible outcome? Suppose that a new mainstreamed student with special learning challenges is placed in your classroom. Part of the teacher's job is to work with the parents and resource staff to identify reasonable educational goals for the student. Without imagination, such goals may be limited or unmotivating to the student. Without discipline, such goals may be unrealistic or may fail to take account of available resources. Imagination that pays attention to real conditions (without being completely beholden to changeable conditions) is most likely to result in the formation of goals that are realistic but also inspiring.

Reference

Dewey, J. 1986. *A common faith.* In *John Dewey: The later works, 1925–1953,* ed. J. A. Boydston, Vol. 9: 1933–1934, 1–60. Carbondale, IL: Southern Illinois University Press.

— ∽ —

John Dewey is surrounded by children for his 90th birthday at the Waldorf Astoria Hotel, October 20, 1949. Among the youngsters are Cricket Rogers, Susan Rogers, Johnny Dewey Jr., and Adrienne Dewey.

A portrait inscribed by Dewey.

Dewey is shown here reading a book.

This photo, published in Saturday Review, *probably was taken toward the end of the 1950s.*

This portrait, inscribed "With love," was taken in the 1930s.

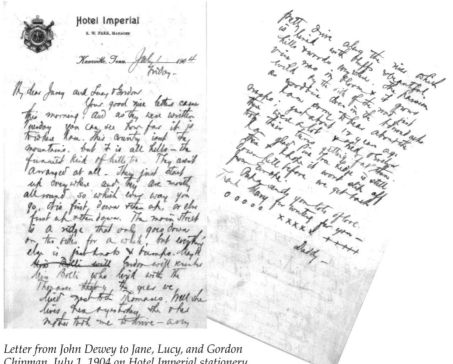

Letter from John Dewey to Jane, Lucy, and Gordon Chipman, July 1, 1904 on Hotel Imperial stationery, Knoxville, Tennessee.
See page 159 for transcript of letter.

Twenty-Eight
Dogma, Democracy, and Education
William G. Wraga

> *Men still want the crutch of dogma, of beliefs fixed by authority, to relieve them of the trouble of thinking and the responsibility of directing their activity by thought. They tend to confine their own thinking to a consideration of which one among the rival systems of dogma they will accept. Hence the schools are better adapted, as John Stuart Mill said, to make disciples than inquirers.*
> —*Democracy and Education*, MW 9: 349

Dewey made this statement in the context of a consideration of the implications of theories of knowledge for education. Specifically, he was concerned that the experimental method was too exclusively associated with scientific and technical branches of knowledge, and insufficiently recognized as a way to inform other kinds of thinking, including "the forming and testing of ideas in social and moral matters" (Dewey 1980, 349). Dewey (1980, 350) expressed concern that schooling had been dominated by "literary, dialectic, and authoritative methods of forming beliefs," beliefs which were rarely if ever tested against logic and evidence, and rather were accepted uncritically and blindly.

Freedoms of Thought and Action

For Dewey, this form of education was antithetical to democracy because it militated against freedom of thought and therefore against the integrity of the individual. For Dewey, in a democracy, the individual enjoyed control over his or her future experience. Dewey maintained that the popular democratic value of freedom of action was meaningful only when accompanied by freedom of thought. Exercised together, these two freedoms would result in intelligent action. Through intelligent action, individuals best controlled subsequent experience. For Dewey, all ideas were subject to analysis and to the ultimate test of practical action. Because dogma involves allegiance to unquestioned intellectual authority, it restricts the free play of intelligence, thereby undermining intelligent action.

Obviously, the frame of mind that Dewey advocated is difficult to cultivate in most people. Most individuals at least attempt to inform their actions with thinking. Yet few of us possess the intellectual courage to submit our most cherished beliefs to reconsideration. For pragmatists like Dewey, even the idea of democracy was subject to continual reevaluation. Contrary to the accusations of many of his critics, Dewey advocated an intellectual education for all future citizens, an education in which students do not merely contemplate big ideas, but one in which they develop the habit of subjecting all ideas to the test of logic and evidence and in which they develop the capacity to apply their intelligence to the resolution of practical problems.

The Dogma of Ideas

How often does this Deweyan form of intellectual citizenship education occur in schools and colleges? From Mill's time to the present, the expectation in many college classrooms is that students will kowtow to the pet theories of the professor. Let us label this practice "the dogma of ideas." Have you seen this kind of dogma in your educational experience? What effect did it have on you? On your classmates? On the attitude and actions of the instructor?

The Dogma of Information

The situation is different in school classrooms, where the emphasis is less on ideas and more on information. Here, typically, teachers deliver prepackaged parcels of facts to students who effectively return them unopened. Opportunities for critical evaluation of ideas or opinions are rare. Inundated with factoids to regurgitate, pupils have little use or even time for the kind of reflection Dewey advocated. Here, the ideas and facts are not tested for truthfulness and usefulness, but students are tested on their uncritical acceptance of the facts as true. Let us call this "the dogma of information." Have you witnessed the dogma of information? How did pupils respond?

The dogma of ideas or the dogma of information—either way, the effect is the same: the teacher postures as an authoritative source of truth. Students are left with the impression that authority figures are absolute in their possession of truth; students learn that the received wisdom from the powers-that-be is to be left unquestioned. This effect not only contradicts Dewey's conception of democracy, but also the constitutional principles of balance of powers and checks and balances: the people are to serve as a check against the official powers-that-be. In short, education in dogma is both anti-intellectual and anti-democratic.

Promoting Independent Thinking

As students, we teachers have no doubt been subject to both the dogma of ideas and the dogma of information. But what can a teacher do to avoid reproducing these kinds of experiences in his or her classroom? Here are several classroom practices that, either directly or indirectly, can promote the kind of independent thinking that Dewey championed. As a teacher, you can convey implicitly to students that authority figures do not necessarily possess authoritative truth; you can do this simply by admitting when you do not know an answer to a student question and by acknowledging when you are mistaken about some matter. Similarly, you can solicit input from students about resolving some classroom difficulty. Routine implementation of these admittedly deceptively simple practices will likely convey implicitly to students a notion of authority consistent with democratic values.

Opportunities for you to foster the kinds of thinking habits that Dewey advocated are plenty, but also depart from the norm in many classrooms, especially in this age when high-stakes testing dominates. Such opportunities range from planning for students to apply subject-related knowledge, skills, and concepts to an evaluation of truth claims (such as news reports related to the subjects you teach), to directly teaching critical thinking skills, to explicitly discussing the issue of dogma in democracy and in education. In the best scenario, you would structure classroom experiences so that students could examine ideas against logic and evidence from all sides. Enact practices like these, and your students will be less likely to end up as disciples and more likely to become inquirers.

Reference

Dewey, J. 1980. *Democracy and education.* In *John Dewey: The middle works, 1899–1924,* ed. J. A. Boydston, Vol. 9: 1916, 1–402. Carbondale, IL: Southern Illinois University Press.

— ∽ —

Twenty-Nine
What to Do? That All Depends

Thomas S. Poetter

> *Truly practical men give their minds free play about a subject without asking too closely at every point for the advantage to be gained; exclusive preoccupation with matters of use and application so narrows the horizon as in the long run to defeat itself. It does not pay to tether one's thoughts to the post of use with too short a rope. Power in action requires some largeness and imaginativeness of vision.*
> —How We Think, MW 6: 289

Practice. Method. Technique. Mechanics. What works?

I've been a "successful" teacher at several levels, with school-age children and with adult learners. As a result of these experiences, I've turned the pursuit of a doctorate in education into a faculty position where I teach teachers. My state and university trust me with novice teachers working on teacher certification and with veteran teachers working on masters and doctoral degrees, even claiming (as do I at times) that I teach them how to teach or to teach better and that I actually do this work quite well.

Ultimately, though, when students of teaching ask me, "What do I do next? Or what would you do next?" regarding a "real" classroom scenario or a hypothetical one, I'm afraid that my responses give little comfort to fledgling practitioners. My response certainly doesn't meet the rigors of accountability the state, no doubt, routinely claims I meet nor does it reflect my supposed levels of expertise, because I always respond, "That depends," because it does.

What Do You Think?

What I would or should do may not be what you would or should do in *every* or even in *any* circumstance. Even if we were somehow in the same setting experiencing the same things, co-teaching if you will, we would have different reactions and actions in response to them. The question, instead, has to be met further with deeper, more critical questions: "What would you do, or better yet, what do you think? AND, don't forget to dream big before you respond or take action." Questions about practice are surely best asked and answered in the context of practicing teaching. Moreover, the pursuit of understanding through thinking and hypothetical imagining are important aspects of teacher education and of a life of fulfilling, reflective professional practice.

This, I know, is quite unsatisfying to beginning teachers who confront real problems in real time when they are out having field experiences and student teaching. They need a chance to voice frustrations and new ideas and to explore their professional selves taking shape. My response "That depends" may suggest that I don't know anything, or that I'm a relativist, or that I don't care about immediate difficulties. Yet I think I do actually know something, and I'm sure I'm no relativist, and I truly do care in the most practical of ways.

Taking an Inquiry Stance

I know what I would do in almost every teaching situation; and even if I can't predict the type of action I would take in every situation (all are different), I know that I would act and that I would do my best to act ethically and on the behalf of students. One problem is that this type of knowledge can't be merely translated. Something else has to happen. We either have to experience the situation together, codeveloping our understanding and repertoires, or we have to trust that over time we'll come to know a range of possibilities for action and be blessed with the imagination and vision to choose well and to extend our students' thinking and achievement beyond our wildest dreams. We must take an inquiry stance to our entire existence, and we can't expect immediate answers to questions that cannot be answered out of context. Remember, no matter how often the establishment tells us that there are particular right answers in teaching, the claims are unsupportable. Experience in teaching bears this out.

Another problem is that unlike their peers in other professional preparation programs in the university, such as pre-law or pre-med or business or nursing, teachers work in a field that offers no clear-cut, scientific set of answers to universal questions. While these other fields have nothing even closely resembling scientific "answers," they teach novices what they do and to act like they do. Their graduates often know a huge body of knowledge and a wide array of "correct" ideas that are universally accepted both conceptually and clinically by the field. They are self-assured, though often wrong; they are confident, though filled with hubris and will commit future disasters because of it. But they are sure, well-armed, oftentimes very capable, and like some beginning teachers, foolish as a result.

In teaching, we ask questions before or after the teaching act like: How much time should I spend on planning and how should I plan? What kinds of materials should I gather? How should I incorporate technology? How will I transform lifeless and boring curriculum materials into experiences that will grab students' interests and tap their concerns? How can I make this lesson sing? And how can I keep Johnny from blurting out? Answers surely can't come easily because they can be answered only with deeper, more critical questions such as: What is your purpose for teaching? What is the purpose of providing a good public education to every citizen? Why do you do the things that you normally do? And how do your decisions to act support and reflect your purposes?

In teacher education, the longer we encourage a focus on issues that are merely technical in teaching, the farther we get from the real possibilities for personal and professional development that teachers need to experience and value in their work. Transforming teaching won't come by focusing on teaching teachers to use certain techniques. How can we expect the public to view us as professionals when the only things we can do or talk about are technical? Our children aren't easily figured out; they are complex. Learning isn't cut-and-dried, but difficult, taxing, and complicated, regardless of how the establishment would have us judge students (on one test score) or teach the curriculum (simply reproducing some-one else's "standards").

Grandness of Vision

Talking about education and teaching takes practice and experience, feedback and extra inquiry; and practicing teaching well, let alone talking about it with some facility, takes grandness of vision—imagination no less. Our best teachers aren't merely technical, by-the-book practitioners. Our best teachers are this and more: They are dreamers who inspire children, parents, and sometimes schools to go far beyond where they thought they could go and to be more than they ever imagined that they could be. Also, they are teachers who gain experience by building a repertoire from day one, experimenting, taking stock, and trying again. They view learning to teach well as a process, not something that gets done once and for all.

Great, imaginative teachers transform the doldrums-filled, standardized, worksheet-driven classroom seizing the day in American public schools. They continue to push students to take on issues around them, address their concerns, and see academic and social knowledge play out in real-world situations around them. These teachers get birthed over a career; they don't get made overnight and aren't "naturals." They work at teaching, developing the "room to maneuver" that allows them the flexibility and expertise to respond adequately without extensive reflection, using their intuition, tacit knowledge, and professional repertoire (Roth 2002). They have a sense of the bigger picture, a commitment to philosophies that work for them, and a foundational ethic to grow over time in competence and skill for the benefit of their students, colleagues, and school. They pay attention to questions deeper than "how to?" Instead they focus on "what?" and "why?" These are the most practical of concerns, and they help us employ the powers of imagination and vision. Great teaching requires no less than a commitment to such grand pursuits.

References

Dewey, J. 1978. *How we think.* In *John Dewey: The middle works, 1899–1924,* ed. J. A. Boydston, Vol. 6: 1910–1911, 177–356. Carbondale, IL: Southern Illinois University Press.

Roth, W.-M. 2002. *Being and becoming in the classroom.* Westport, CT: Ablex.

Thirty
The Teacher as Theorist and Lover

Greg Seals

> *Theory is in the end, as has been well said, the most practical of all things, because this widening of range of attention beyond nearby purpose and desire eventually results in the creation of wider and farther-reaching purposes.*
>
> —*The Sources of a Science of Education*, LW 5: 8

Love, any number of sages would like us to believe, is the most impractical of matters. Love has been compared variously, and by and large unfavorably, to a sweet young dream, a frailty of mind, a purplish wound, and, to paraphrase the Scottish poet James Hogg, "a dizziness that will not let poor bodies go about their bizziness." But anyone who has experienced love knows differently, and better. Over the course of love, we come to recognize the fact that it is love that puts us in touch with what is real, clarifies mind and purpose, contributes to a wholeness and soundness of soul, and establishes equilibrium in the progress of our lives.

As it is with love, so it is with theory. Theory makes it possible for us to interact with the world on more intimate terms. Theories connect isolated facts, as Dewey (1984, 11) argued in *The Sources of a Science of Education*, into a system, a science:

> *The practitioner who knows the system and its laws is evidently in possession of a powerful instrument for observing and interpreting what goes on before him. This intellectual tool affects his attitudes and modes of response in what he does. Because the range of understanding is deepened and widened he can take into account remote consequences which were originally hidden from view and hence ignored in his actions. Greater continuity is introduced; he does not isolate situations and deal with them in separation as he was compelled to do when ignorant of connecting principles. At the same time, his practical dealings become more flexible. Seeing more relations he sees more possibilities, more opportunities. He is emancipated from the need of following tradition and special precedents. His ability to judge being enriched, he has a wider range of alternatives to select from in dealing with individual situations.*

In possession of a theory, simple, stagnant *seeing* becomes superabundant, superlatively significant *seeing as*. Ordinary things take on beautiful shapes and wondrous forms they did not possess prior to their appearance in the light shed by the theory. The practitioner with a theory begins to recognize the value and importance of experimenting with, and even romancing, ideas.

Through the Lens of a Theory

Applied more specifically to education, Dewey takes the teacher with a theory to be entirely changed in his or her attitudes and intentions, professional habits of inquiry, observations, and interpretations. Looking at schooling through the lens of a theory enables educators to recognize new problems, devise new procedures, and diversify their understanding and approach to their practical, pedagogical tasks. Ideational interaction with the world of schooling takes on a freer, even flirtatious form for the teacher who is also a theorist of education. What is more, the world, when treated in this manner, magically it would seem, learns to reciprocate in kind.

Loving What You Do

Because he or she has a theory, the scientist, like the lover, is able to see every-where signs of his or her beloved. If this is true, then the conclusion is obvious. Dewey's apparent paradox about theory being ultimately the most practical of all things is easily resolved by realizing a perfectly clear truth. Having a theory about what you are doing is a way of loving what you do. The difference to everyday action between loving what you do and not loving what you do is so great that it seems entirely correct to say that Dewey was right. There may, after all, be no matter of greater possible practical importance than theory.

Reference

Dewey, J. 1984. *The sources of a science of education*. In *John Dewey: The later works, 1925–1953*, ed. J. A. Boydston, Vol. 5: 1929–1930, 1–40. Carbondale, IL: Southern Illinois University Press.

— ∽ —

Thirty-One
The Role of Intelligence in the Creation of Art

Elliot W. Eisner

> Any idea that ignores the necessary role of intelligence in the production of works of art is based upon identification of thinking with use of one special kind of material, verbal signs and words. To think effectively in terms of relations of qualities is as severe a demand upon thought as to think in terms of symbols, verbal and mathematical. Indeed, since words are easily manipulated in mechanical ways, the production of a work of genuine art probably demands more intelligence than does most of the so-called thinking that goes on among those who pride themselves on being 'intellectuals.'
> —*Art as Experience*, LW 10: 52

The foregoing quotation from Dewey's *Art as Experience* has profound impli-cations for the ways in which we conceptualize mind and its engine, intelligence. For Dewey, intelligence was not a quantity of something one possesses, but the qualities of a process intended to realize some worthwhile aim. The concept of intelligence as a process undermines a view that conceives of intelligence as something that is physical, an entity genetically conferred, something that can be discovered, mapped, and measured.

The qualification that intelligence must be directed toward worthwhile ends is also of consequence for it emphasizes the point that mere cleverness, canniness, shrewdness that leads to nefarious conduct is not, and cannot be, a mark of intelligence for it neglects the larger consequence to which nefarious modes of thinking ultimately lead. Put most simply, burglars, as Dewey reminded us in *Experience and Education* (1988), do not function as intelligent beings.

Qualities of Intelligence

The association of intelligence with the process of creating art is one that is seldom explored by those studying intelligence. Intelligence, as Dewey suggested, is typically believed to be situated in the use of words and numbers. Consider both the scholastic achievement test and the graduate record exam as examples of instruments that, among other things, attempt to assess the intellectual ability of students and their readiness for college or graduate school. The ability to create images in sound and in sight are not included in the data that are used to make judgments about college admission.

The implicit message is that being smart means being smart with words and numbers. Thus, what Dewey gave us is a reconceptualization of intelligence, one that not only emphasizes its process features, one that not only points out its connection to moral considerations, but also one that expands the concept of intelligence so that it includes the selection and organization of qualities as well as the selection and use of symbols, verbal and mathematical.

Smart in Different Ways

Dewey advanced this view in 1934, well before conceptions of multiple intelligences and other efforts to diversify the concept emerged in the psychological and educational literature. Dewey recognized that people were smart in different ways—some in social situations, others in theoretical matters, still others in the arena of the arts.

The implications of this view for school practice are enormous. If we took his views seriously at a practical level, we would be acknowledging the significance of intelligence in all of its varieties and we would be providing opportunities in school for their cultivation. At the moment, individuals smart in ways that schools neglect do not secure opportunities to secure a place in the sun. Our views of human intelligence are limited by comparison, despite the fact that Dewey's ideas on this matter are almost three-quarters of a century old.

Ultimately, educational equity requires opportunities for students to follow their bliss, to pursue the realization of their talents, to develop the forms of thought and human intelligence for which they have a special affinity. Dewey provided an early frame of reference for thinking about such matters. It remains for those of us in education to muster the will and the energy to shape educational policies and to structure schools so that the ideals Dewey expressed can be realized in the lives that students lead.

Reference

Dewey, J. 1987. *Art as experience*. In *John Dewey: The later works, 1925–1953*, ed. J. A. Boydston, Vol. 10: 1934, 1–456. Carbondale, IL: Southern Illinois University Press.

Dewey, J. 1988. *Experience and education*. In *John Dewey: The later works, 1925–1953*, ed. J. A. Boydston, Vol. 13: 1938–1939, 1–62. Carbondale, IL: Southern Illinois University Press.

Thirty-Two

Autonomous Education: Free to Determine Its Own Ends

Larry A. Hickman

> *Until educators get the independence and courage to insist that educational aims are to be formed as well as executed within the educative process, they will not come to consciousness of their own function. Others will then have no great respect for educators because educators do not respect their own social place and work.*
> —The Sources of a Science of Education, LW 5: 38

These two sentences are among the most important that Dewey wrote. They occupy a place at the heart of one of his most important statements about education. Even so, they are in some ways quite surprising—almost absurd, as he would later say—because they contain implicit warnings against several widely accepted ideas.

Implicit Warnings

First, we should not allow social conditions to determine our educational values and practices. When educational values and practices fall prey to ideological constraints, whether political or religious, they inevitably fail. When educational values and practices are called upon to reflect community values, they risk default. And when educational values and practices are subsumed to the demands of industry and commerce, they have lost their bearings. Society is a product of education; it does not furnish a standard for educational values and practices.

Second, we should not think that educational values and practices can be determined solely by educational researchers. Educational research can furnish many useful tools by which many educational values and practices can be reconfigured to meet changed and changing conditions. Educational research can provide teachers with inspiration to get through difficult times in the classroom by offering fresh perspectives on old problems. And educational research can help us as teachers think more clearly about our work by locating specific issues in a broader context. But educational research only can provide tools; it cannot determine the specifics of how they are to be used.

Third, and perhaps most surprisingly, we should not think that educational values and practices are determined by us as teachers. As teachers, it is proper and even inevitable that we bring our own ideals and methods to the classroom. But also important is that our ideals and methods be refined and reconfigured by means of the educative process. As teachers, we may be at the heart of the educational process, but we are not the process itself.

Fourth, and finally, the tests we administer to our students must be carefully designed so that they do not interfere with or supplant the educative process. We must remember that IQ tests and other standardized tests tend to focus on only one of many variables to the exclusion of others that may be of equal or greater importance. The educative process demands that a broad range of factors be taken into account. It is easy to forget that tests are by their very nature theoretical exercises; they must not be taken as indicating something final, but only as a source of data for further investigation.

Educational Values and Practices

In short, what Dewey called the *educative process* determines educational values and practices. The norms of education cannot be conveyed in "cookbook" fashion, nor in books of lists. They emerge, instead, as teachers interact with students in the process of learning. Education—the educative process—is autonomous, Dewey reminded us. In a robust democracy, it must be free to determine its own ends.

These are complex ideas. They conflict with accepted wisdom and practice, and they are extremely challenging to implement. The influences of social conditions, educational research, the backgrounds and interests of teachers, and standardized testing are often so strong that looking beyond these factors to focus on the educative process itself is difficult. Nevertheless, only by maintaining such a focus can social conditions, educational research, our efforts as teachers, and educational testing enjoy continued reconstruction and renewal.

Reference

Dewey, J. 1984. *The sources of a science of education.* In *John Dewey: The later works, 1925–1953*, ed. J. A. Boydston, Vol. 5: 1929–1930, 1–40. Carbondale, IL: Southern Illinois University Press.

— ∽ —

PART V
DEMOCRATIC
CITIZENSHIP

Preparing Children for Democratic Citizenship

Rick Breault

Little in the typical teacher-preparation program encourages teachers to think about what it means to prepare children for democratic citizenship. You can search the various teacher standards, regardless of their acronyms (NCATE, INTASC, NBPTS, PDS), and you will not find any emphasis on preparing young people for a life in democratic society. You might find something in the social studies content area standards or some references in the general standards to nurturing qualities that are implicit in good democratic citizens, but nothing that mentions democratic citizenship as such. Once you get into the school environment itself, things are even worse. Any deliberate discussion of schooling for democracy has been nearly completely drowned out by the rallying cry, "Get a score and get a job!" Dewey would not be pleased.

This final set of reflections is intended to leave you with a challenge. If you read only the preceding four parts, there is the possibility that you will walk away with a better, but incomplete understanding of Dewey's purpose. The intellectual development of individual students was certainly a concern for Dewey. However, he reminded us in Democracy and Education (1980, 16):

> *A being connected with other beings cannot perform his own activities without taking the activities of others into account. For they are indispensable conditions of the realization of his tendencies. When he moves he stirs them and reciprocally.*

And later in that same book, Dewey (1980, 92) told us:

> *The essential point is that isolation makes for rigidity and formal institutionalizing of life, for static and selfish ideals within the group.*

Educating for Democratic Citizenship

Dewey was seldom more clear or definitive on a point than he was when explaining that we cannot help but live in society, and society is most effective when it is lived as a democracy. Dewey's vision of educating for democratic citizenship, however, bears little resemblance to the simplistic version we currently see in most schools, or what I call the "3 Ps"—be productive (get a job), be patriotic (say the Pledge of Allegiance), and participate (vote).

Even in some of the better curricula, democratic citizenship is something that you learn *about* so you can participate later in life. It is an established body of knowledge or set of behaviors you learn so that you can be a better citizen. If democracy is practiced at all in the classroom, it is usually in the form of voting on choices determined by the teacher or maybe developing classroom rules together. While the latter is not a bad idea, it focuses on society's role in controlling its citizens rather than releasing their potential.

What you will read in the following selections should both trouble and excite you. Dewey pulls no punches in describing the school's responsibility in nurturing democratic citizenship, and it is not an easy task. Consider these words from *The School and Society* (1976, 10):

> *We must conceive of them [school work] in their social significance, as types of the processes by which society keeps itself going, as agencies for bringing home to the child some of the primal necessities of community life . . . in short, as instrumentalities through which the school itself shall be made a genuine form of active community life, instead of a place set apart to learn lessons.*

A Dynamic Process

Where Dewey differs from what we currently call education for democracy is in his emphasis on democracy and democratic education, not as established content but as a dynamic process. The community and the school always must be asking: What kind of society do we want and what kind of school will help bring about that society? This idea permeates Dewey's (1980, 103) writing (all emphases have been added):

> *The conception of education as* a social process *and function has no definite meaning until we define the kind of society we have in mind. Democracy is the faith that the* process of experience is more important *than any special results attained, so that special results achieved are of ultimate value* only as they are used to enrich and order the ongoing process.

Dewey would not oppose the idea of preparing young people for the world of work. In fact, he would encourage it. However, there is an important difference between a curriculum that helps children become integrated into the working life of the community and one that is narrowly focused on careerism and stresses simply getting a job, especially if that emphasis leads to the perpetuation of a privileged class and a more limited curriculum "conceived for the masses" (Dewey 1980, 200). He might also have a problem with the understanding of democracy and economics that is currently dominant in our schools, and culture in general, which emphasizes individualistic consumerism as an expression of freedom.

Where we currently have "token economies" in which young children are "paid" or rewarded with trinkets from the school store for doing their schoolwork, Dewey would have us provide meaningful and productive activities that students would want to do for their intrinsic reward. While the present trend in field trips is to visit toy and sporting good stores—paid for by those stores— Dewey might have suggested visiting local craftspeople and small factories to see the importance and contribution of work and cooperation in the life of the community. The emphasis would be better placed on the ingenuity of the creative process and what the individual contributes to communal life than on helping to create early brand loyalty to a mega-corporation that might well have rent the fabric of the local community by driving small business owners into bankruptcy or sending local factory jobs overseas.

Preparing Students for Democratic Living

Yes, you will find that this part presents quite a challenge. To prepare your students for democratic living, you must allow them to live democratically. That means you will need to implement a curriculum that takes into consideration everything you have read to this point. Classrooms that model thoughtful, participatory democratic living are characterized by experiences that focus on active learning, meaningful inquiry, and critical thinking. If all this sounds overwhelming, and it probably does, keep in mind that Dewey also described democracy and education as a process in which we move gradually toward the kind of society—or classroom—we seek. To conclude with Dewey's (1987, 219) own words:

> *The foundation of democracy is faith in the capacities of human nature; faith in human intelligence and in the power of pooled and cooperative experience. It is not belief that these things are complete but that, if given a show, they will grow and be able to generate progressively the knowledge and wisdom needed to guide collective action.*

References

Dewey, J. 1976. *The school and society.* In *John Dewey: The middle works, 1899–1924,* ed. J. A. Boydston, Vol. 1: 1899–1901, 1–112. Carbondale, IL: Southern Illinois University Press.

Dewey, J. 1980. *Democracy and education.* In *John Dewey: The middle works, 1899–1924,* ed. J. A. Boydston, Vol. 9: 1916, 1–402. Carbondale, IL: Southern Illinois University Press.

Dewey, J. 1987. *Democracy and educational administration.* In *John Dewey: The later works, 1925–1953,* ed. J. A. Boydston, Vol. 11: 1935–1937, 217–25. Carbondale, IL: Southern Illinois University Press.

— ∽ —

Thirty-Three
Teaching Democracy for Life

John M. Novak

> *Democracy is a way of life controlled by a working faith in the possibilities of human nature.*
> —Creative Democracy: The Task Before Us, LW 14: 226

Teaching in and for a democracy is a daunting and creative challenge. It is much more than emphasizing the importance of voting or being informed about the governmental process. Both of these are important, but democracy goes much deeper than that. Teaching in and for a democracy is about learning to live a shared life and finding ways to grow through meaningful participation in important social issues.

Democracy as a way of life emphasizes that people grow as they learn to bring their individuality and intelligence to the many communities they inhabit. Human growth and development do not come merely from the inside or the outside. That is, human beings do not have a specific inborn human potential that emerges regardless of what happens in their environment. Neither are they blank

115

slates that are mechanically stamped out by their surroundings. Individuals and their communities grow as a result of the unique contributions people bring to group tasks and challenges. Through this give-and-take process, individuals learn to understand the perspectives of other people and develop one another's ability to be heard and taken seriously.

Participative Living

Teaching for a democratic way of life means being able to model this way of participative living. Teachers realize that students attend not only to what they say but, more importantly, to what they do. A democratic way of living requires that teachers and students engage in a "doing with" relationship. The lived experience of this "doing with" relationship communicates the message that "we are all in this together."

Looked at metaphorically, this way of teaching should be more like participating in a jazz band than marching in a drum and bugle corps. In the latter, people are interchangeable parts that follow a set of specific instructions to arrive at a predetermined goal. Though there may be energetic engagement, the process is closed—participants are merely following orders. The job of the teacher is to make sure that everyone stays in line and is in the right place at the right time.

In a jazz band, individuals participate in a developing theme that is enhanced by their anticipated creative extensions. Participants are expected to want to be competent, committed, and creative. The job of the teacher is to make this metaphorical possibility a creative reality. The role involves, on the one hand, knowing who your students are and where their interests and talents lie. On the other hand, the role means having a solid grasp of what you are teaching and the creative possibilities that exist in connecting subject matter with individual student interests and abilities. This role develops by having a feel for your students and your subject matter, and possessing the artistic desire and competence to bring them together in vitally enhancing ways.

Positive Possibilities

There is no guarantee that this jazz-like effect will occur in its most artistic form every time a teacher encounters a class. This is not an all-or-nothing affair, but has a better chance of developing if it is a part of a melioristic faith in human possibility. Seasoned meliorism for democratic teachers needs to be distinguished from naïve optimism and cynical pessimism. The former implies that good things will result regardless of what we do as teachers. The latter perspective is resigned to the belief that teaching cannot make any real difference in people's lives. The mistake of both of these positions is that they imply that good or bad things are guaranteed regardless of a teacher's actions. A seasoned meliorism necessary for democratic living is based on the idea that jazz-like encounters are more apt to develop if teachers approach teaching and learning situations with an energetic openness to positive possibilities and reflectively learn from previous and present experiences.

A working faith in human nature is a stance from which a teacher operates. In baseball, a batter digs in and takes his or her stance. Stances can differ, but their aim is to enable the batter to make a solid connection with the ball. Good hitters modify their stance according to previous experience and current conditions. Similarly, a democratic teacher digs in with a stance that is built on a working faith in human possibilities. This working faith says that all people are valuable, able, and responsible and can behave accordingly in cooperative and collaborative activities. Enacting this stance is not easy and does not negate the fact that people may at times be apathetic, self-centered, or narrow-minded in their actions. At the very least, a working faith in human possibilities assumes that human nature is not fundamentally evil, that social life can be filled with meaningful encounters, that intelligence can handle more complex problems, and that teachers can learn from successful and unsuccessful endeavors. This working faith in human nature points a teacher in the right direction and enables self-correcting strategies to develop.

Modeling Democratic Living

Teachers need to model this democratic stance outside as well as inside the classroom. In the governance of their school, teachers should be active leaders for democratic living. Their voices need to be heard and artfully combined as they participate in a creative endeavor to make their school a model for creative democratic processes. Connecting the school to the larger outside world, this working faith in human nature means that teachers also attend to the societal resources, strategies, and commitments that make this way of life available to all.

A commitment to a democratic way of life is not easy and is never finished. But what is the alternative for creative and committed teachers in a democratic society? The democratic teachers I have encountered have found ways to grow personally and professionally in bringing this ideal to life and in bringing life to this ideal.

Reference

Dewey, J. 1988. Creative democracy: The task before us. In *John Dewey: The later works, 1925–1953*, ed. J. A. Boydston, Vol. 14: 1939–1941, 224–30. Carbondale, IL: Southern Illinois University Press.

— ∞ —

Thirty-Four
John Dewey and the American Creed

Daniel Tanner

> *It should be a commonplace, but unfortunately it is not, that no education—or anything else for that matter—is progressive unless it is making progress.*
> —Introduction to *The Use of Resources in Education*, ix

So wrote John Dewey in his last piece of published writing before his death on June 1, 1952. In his last work, Dewey reviewed some of the successes of progressive education, but also noted the lack of progress in many quarters, and the difficult road ahead for the democratic transformation of school and society. There, he (1952, viii) pointed to the difficulties of recent years in which "organized attacks on the achievements of progressive education have become more extensive and virulent than ever before."

Fallacies and Failures of Dualistic Thinking

For Dewey, the progressive education movement, as part of a wider democratic social movement, never can rest as long as it is committed to the improvement of the human condition. Throughout his life, he exposed the contradictions and conflicts of dualistic thinking in impeding the method of intelligence and preventing problem resolution and solution. He prophetically exposed the Soviet fallacy in holding that democratic ends would emerge from undemocratic means. He exposed the erroneous belief that restrictions on civil liberties are necessary to protect American democracy and that gains in social welfare are made at the expense of individuality. In the present-day wake of international terrorism, the American public is led by its leaders to believe that security can be protected only through sacrifices in civil freedoms. But Dewey made it clear that democracy is the best guarantor of freedom and security.

Dewey advanced the needed interdependence of knowledge and exposed the hazards of knowledge dualism—such as the divorce between the sciences and humanities—decades before C. P. Snow (1959) addressed the issue and exposed its inevitable losses to humanity when the branches of knowledge are isolated or set against one another.

He forewarned researchers in the behavioral sciences against setting a divide between the qualitative and quantitative research in educational investigation. Early in the 20th century, he held that all research must be grounded in an intellectually coherent and inclusive system of ideas and quality, and must employ appropriate techniques if the results are to attain generalized significance.

Nature of the Learner

Dewey orchestrated a theory of democracy and education on a global scale. Yet some of his deepest and most far-reaching insights and realizations on human nature and behavior grew out of his observations of children in his laboratory school. Just imagine a curriculum built upon what Dewey identified as the four impulses of children—the social, the investigative, the constructive, and the expressive/artistic—or what may be termed the fourfold functions of developmental learning.

Dewey anticipated Piaget by decades—and he went further, for he systematically interrelated the design and function of the school curriculum to child and adolescent development. He anticipated and contributed to the emergence of modern cognitive/developmental psychology in answer to the warring sects in psychology that impeded progress in understanding the nature of the learner in a free society.

Transformation of the Curriculum into the Working Powers of Intelligence

Dewey systematically conceived of and demonstrated the means for constructing the school curriculum to advance the learners' growth. He explained the processes of reflective thinking and the method of intelligence for social and personal problem solving necessary for productive citizenship in a democracy. He conceived of education as the process through which experience is reconstructed for growth—both in the meaning of experience and in advancing the ability to direct the course of subsequent experience. He held that the process of education must empower the learner in the control of his or her destiny by transforming the curriculum into the working power of intelligence. Dewey provided educators with a paradigm revealing how the success or failure of educational reform hinges on the extent to which the curriculum is in harmony with the nature and needs of the learner and the democratic prospect.

Many authorities on Dewey fail or refuse to recognize that what they regard as his greatest single work, *Democracy and Education* (1980), originally published in 1916, systematically integrated educational theory and democracy through the very structure and function of the school curriculum. Indeed, he defined philosophy as the general theory of education. Through education and its agency of curriculum, the rising generation develops its fundamental intellectual, emotional, and instrumental dispositions toward life in all of its manifestations.

Education and the American Creed

More than any other figure of the past century, Dewey promoted and strengthened the belief in education as the principal conclusion of the American Creed (Myrdal 1962). Among the multitude of cultures that find conflict in American and global society, Dewey envisioned an overarching intercultural education to build a sense of unity through diversity.

He conceived of community not as a group set against other groups by special interests, but as a cosmopolitan association of people who draw their strength through finding common cause in their diverse talents. He never doubted the democratic prospect and was an activist for virtually every democratic social movement—educational opportunity, human rights, child welfare, academic freedom, and social justice. He advised his fellow philosophers that they should study the problems of humanity rather than the problems of philosophy.

Throughout his life and over the course of a half-century since his passing, Dewey has been vilified, honored, betrayed, vindicated, attacked, and defended. But when all is said and done, he gave America and the world the most provocative, comprehensive, and powerful vision for human progress through democracy and education for the 21st century. He was a man for his times and a man for all times. He knew full well that progress is never made. By its very nature, progress is in the making.

119

References

Dewey, J. 1952. Introduction. In *The use of resources in education,* by Clapp, vii–xi. New York: Harper and Row.

Dewey, J. 1980. *Democracy and education.* In *John Dewey: The middle works, 1899–1924,* ed. J. A. Boydston, Vol. 9: 1916, 1–402. Carbondale, IL: Southern Illinois University Press.

Myrdal, G. 1962. *An American dilemma,* 20th anniversary ed. New York: Harper and Row.

Snow, C. P. 1959. *The two cultures and the scientific revolution.* New York: Cambridge University Press.

—— ∽ ——

Thirty-Five
Realizing a Common Good

Randy Hewitt

> *The desired transformation is not difficult to define in a formal way. It signifies a society in which every person shall be occupied in something which makes the lives of others better worth living, and which accordingly makes the ties which bind persons together more perceptible—which breaks down the barriers of distance between them.*
> —Democracy and Education, MW 9: 326

As Dewey professed, life means growth, development, and change over time. However, simply to say that life means growth tells us nothing about the extent, intensity, and content of this growth as it takes concrete form.

To ask what life *is* at any one moment in time, to inquire into growth as it takes shape and develops qualitative characteristics, is to ask an empirical question. To ask what concrete form life *should* take, to ask in what direction and how growth *should* proceed, is to ask a philosophical question. To be concerned with the philosophical question is to be concerned with what kind of individual and community *should* be in the making. It is to take a conscious interest in what ends *should* guide individuals' growth in shared experience. Furthermore, it is to be concerned with the capacities, skills, affections, and dispositions necessary to realize these ends.

Desirable Ends

If philosophy serves as the means by which we imagine a better state of human affairs from the one that now exists, then education serves as the means by which we deliberately bring this better state of affairs into being. Philosophy, then, identifies the desirable ends within individual and social growth, and thus defines the aims and purposes of education.

What does it mean to say that the aim of education should be to bring about "a society in which every person shall be occupied in something which makes the lives of others better worth living, and which accordingly makes the ties which bind persons together more perceptible—which breaks down the barriers of distance between them"? Furthermore, why should this be the aim of education? To answer these two questions, it is necessary to sketch out the philosophical foundation that gives warrant to this aim of education.

Shared Activities

Human beings unavoidably share in concrete activities that yield concrete results. That is, an individual's environment always includes other human beings already engaged in activities ("occupations," as Dewey sometimes called them) aimed at common ends. Therefore, any individual's particular tendencies of action are inextricably social and thus are socially cultivated and learned activities.

Simply put, shared activities provide human beings with the fundamental means of living and learning. They supply specific ends, aims, and purposes for human conduct through which individuals first develop interest, desire, judgment, and motive. Shared activities stimulate, organize, and direct individuals' senses, attention, and motion. Shared activities provoke thought and incite emotion necessary for personal—and social—growth. They are the essential substances through which individuals acquire and refine their special affections, dexterities, and aptitudes. In short, shared activities are organs of intelligence. They form the central nerves whereby the individual not only develops specific tendencies to act, but also more or less realizes his or her inherent connection to others as an indispensable condition for nourishing personal growth.

Shared activities, furthermore, help form the moral fiber or character of the individual. They serve as the medium through which the individual filters the demands of others on himself or herself and refines personal abilities in light of their claims. Because the individual must continue enlisting the support of others for growth, he or she must develop some degree of interest in their modes of response and their expectations of the consequences as a result of these responses. If he or she is to acquire the skills necessary to become a part of the group, he or she must assimilate not only its likes, dislikes, desires, purposes, and plans, but also its demands that these plans be carried out in particular ways.

Others command the individual to consider the significance of his or her actions more carefully. They demand that an individual develop his or her interests and act in a way that is considerate of others as they attempt to develop their own interests. As claims of right, their expectations sharpen judgment about the direction and control over specific desires and inspire and enlarge the individual's idea of the good to be served. In a general, more formal way, shared activities provide the individual with an intrinsic ideal for conduct that serves as both a good and standard.

As the good or aim of conduct, the ideal refers to the individual's conscious tendency to develop his or her particular capacities and interests *in harmony* with the demands and needs of others as they develop their own powers. From the point of view of the self, the goal of any activity or occupation is to act in such a way that will improve one's interests, skills, desires, attitudes, habits, and judgment. From the social point of view, the goal is to act in such a way that will improve the specific shared conditions (the arrangements, opportunities, and materials) that nourish the activities and growth of others.

As a standard of judgment, the ideal refers to the degree to which the individual actually brings about this harmony by acting upon his or her conception of good. In their attempts to realize a common good through their various activities, individuals come to share lives and communicate with one another in more intimate and varied ways. As a result, they come to learn from one another. They come to identify new interests and capacities for further growth, as well as responsibilities intrinsic to these new potentials. Thus, the ideal of self-growth inherent to shared activities entails two principles whose just relation makes up the democratic ideal: individual liberty and social equality.

Social Experience

An enriched democratic experience, however, cannot be secured merely by virtue of collective acceptance and general appeal to its abstract principles. The work of democracy can be made concrete, secured, refined, and extended only through the day-in and day-out activities that human beings share. Democracy as a moral ideal challenges each individual to be actively engaged with the particular problems that arise within his or her shared occupations and that limit free and full contact with others. Only through active concern for the community can problems be immediately felt, understood, and appreciated with sympathy. Only through constant communication, persistent questioning, and critical reflection about shared ends and purposes, and the special needs and capacities of all involved, can existing efforts to satisfy social needs be measured, deficiencies be identified, and further work be suggested.

A flourishing democratic experience requires free flowing and broad communication about the consequences of shared activities. Mutual reference and exchange of ideas is vital to making "the ties which bind persons together more perceptible," for multiplying perceptions of possible human resources, sharpening consciousness of shared ends, and stoking the desire to excel beyond existing conceptions of good. Constant vigilance over existing efforts to meet social demands helps detect conditions that set up unequal relations of power and stifle human interaction and freedom of individual growth. An education most fitting to democracy is one that consciously aims to cultivate what Dewey (1980, 15) called "robust trustees of its own resources and ideals."

Education, in the most general sense, is the means by which a democratic society consciously modifies itself to enhance the depth and range of shared meaning and bring about a more unified social experience. In light of the philosophical foundation stated here, education should entail the cultivation of democratically minded individuals charged with the responsibility of bringing about a more intimate, harmonious experience. Therefore, the aim of instruction is to develop democratic characters who are socially and politically engaged according to their own specific interests.

Good teaching, then, aims to provide the experiences necessary to direct individuals, on their own, to sense, test, measure, reflect upon, and develop an idea of their experiences. Put differently, good teaching cultivates the emotional and intellectual powers of attention, perception, memory, imagination, conception, and judgment in individuals such that they widen and enrich the significance of their own interests by reference to the interests and needs of others. Fundamentally, the aim of instruction is to develop in students the affections, sympathies, and conceptual habits necessary for critical analysis of ideas and assumptions that work to preclude or enhance a more intimate experience with others.

Reference

Dewey, J. 1980. *Democracy and education.* In *John Dewey: The middle works, 1899–1924,* ed. J. A. Boydston, Vol. 9: 1916, 1–402. Carbondale, IL: Southern Illinois University Press.

— ∽ —

Thirty-Six
Teacher as Shaper of Social Process

Louise M. Berman

> *The conception of education as a social process and function has no definite meaning until we define the kind of society we have in mind.*
> —*Democracy and Education,* MW 9: 103

Business cannot be as usual! Changes in society for good and for bad have suddenly brought the realization that we live in a relatively small global village. And, in this village, we see:

- increasing gaps between the haves and the have nots;
- insecurity about the varieties of ways life can be diminished or extinguished through terrorist attacks;
- inadequate access by many to both medicine and medical services;
- school systems with little teaching of our democratic heritage or possibilities;
- lack of will on the parts of many persons to become politically active in causes beyond those that have an immediate impact upon themselves;
- the tendency of people to fill their lives with endless activity without giving adequate attention to what really matters; and
- lack of reflection because of a surfeit of information and choice.

People today are faced with multilayered problems, as well as possibilities; therefore, they may give inadequate attention to that spirit and vision which has inspired persons for generations. Dewey probably would ask us to consider the kind of society we have in mind, just as he raised that question in the 1940s.

One way of dealing with societal vision and purpose might be the constant refinement of the meaning of *social process.* The term lends itself to considering a variety of topics that might be included in a society's statement of purpose. How a society views the social processes it seeks to teach, or neglects to teach, its young partially determines the direction of that society.

Creating a Societal Vision

That Dewey was concerned about constant change and reform suggests that no one statement of the ends of society will be complete. Within Dewey's philosophy, such a statement constantly will be shaped and reshaped. Allow me then to raise a few questions about education that teachers, students, parents, and concerned citizens might ponder and act upon as they think about the kind of society they wish for themselves and others.

What thoughts, ideas, and values energize teachers and others interested in thinking about the process of finding some common perspectives? A dynamic society is not a ho-hum entity. Teachers and others bring to their settings themselves as persons. Each individual, therefore, must reflect upon that which makes him or her a fully functioning human being so that the excitement, newness, and considered values of each person are inviting to human contact, communication, and connection. The teacher who is vibrant and sharing of a considered self is attractive to other human beings. Teaching and learning are then fostered through both indirect and direct means.

How do we establish contexts, including schools and classrooms, so that mini-communities are formed? In such communities, social processes are taught. These processes might include, but are not limited to, sharing power, showing compassion to others like and unlike one's self, using minds actively, searching for just and moral means of dealing with human problems, uncovering goodness in people's actions, and teaching civility as a way of honoring and respecting the opinions of others.

How will persons learn to make a difference in the various communities in which they are involved? Possibilities for such action will vary depending on the ages of the students, the nature of the context, and the yearnings of the people within the community to help bring about needed societal changes. The key is to provide settings in which persons can identify problems and dilemmas and work on them in concert. Questions might be addressed, such as: How can persons learn to exercise political power by communicating with different kinds of persons, asking piercing questions, mediating conflicting ideas and ideologies, and showing civility, compassion, and concern in difficult situations? What does it take to stay with a tough project until some resolution is achieved? For example, volunteerism is sometimes part of school programs. Such activities help individual students develop certain ways of showing interest in others and fine-tuning intellectual and emotional skills. But when fundamental societal change is a major purpose, students must learn political skills of negotiation, conflict resolution, and consensus building. How can additional skills be built into an existing program?

How will teachers and leaders help students and their communities to develop the will to think about fresh priorities in society and schools? For example, what can be deleted from the curriculum to make time and space for the enhancement of knowledge, skills, and feelings necessary to our living together harmoniously? How do we use these skills to encourage better schools for all children or more adequate health services for poor neighborhoods or countries?

How can schools and communities interact so that the quality of life for all is enhanced? For example, in neighborhoods with students from diverse political, socioeconomic, and ethnic backgrounds, conversations between school personnel and neighbors invite parties to hear the background and purposes of one another. Schools may help through their attempts to look for commonalities and differences in neighborhood diversity. We seem to have done well in acknowledging diversity, but perhaps we have to search for fresh ways to talk about our common humanity.

How do the academic disciplines contribute to students' building of projects based upon life in their mini-communities? Geography, history, philosophy, literature, mathematics, the arts, physical education, and the sciences all provide insights and ways of thinking that are important to Dewey's focus on mind as capable of continuous growth, integration, and change. While Dewey's thinking about organized subjects is sometimes misunderstood, he strongly emphasized the use of the disciplines in learning how to live well, solve problems, and live ethically with others. The disciplines provide incentives for imagining the lives of others, making extraordinary observations, engaging in creative renderings of thought, and judging with exquisite sensitivity.

How do we as teachers help persons learn to live with the uncertain, the ambiguous, and conflicting perspectives as students search for answers to perplexing questions? Perhaps one of the most important and compelling aspects of teaching is helping persons live imaginatively and wisely in a world full of contradictions and unanswerable questions. Providing settings where students look for alternative possibilities and connections among contending points of view may enhance their ability to live with joy and satisfaction in a world of perplexities and paradoxes.

Paying Attention to What Needs Fixing

Education is not business as usual. I started this reflection with a number of societal changes that need attention. Clearly, I could list numerous things that are good in our world and immediate society. Ignoring the problems, though, is dangerous. When the brakes or transmission in a car begin to give out, the persons in it are in trouble. Unless we pay attention to what needs fixing, all of us may suffer.

Teachers and communities need to work out the meanings of social process for the settings of which they are part. Such action involves looking and relooking, creating and re-creating answers to society's toughest problems. Such action involves the joy and suffering that frequently accompany newness of ideas and activity. Such action involves naming those attitudes, predispositions, and learnings to live amicably with self and others. Such actions mean persons reaching beyond themselves to apply learnings from their immediate context to the world community with its problems begging for solutions.

So let's get started in the contexts within which each of us works.

Reference

Dewey, J. 1980. *Democracy and education*. In *John Dewey: The middle works, 1899–1924*, ed. J. A. Boydston, Vol. 9: 1916, 1–402. Carbondale, IL: Southern Illinois University Press.

— ᗡᗡ —

Thirty-Seven

Foundations of Deweyan Democracy: Human Nature, Intelligence, and Cooperative Inquiry

Stephen M. Fishman

> *The foundation of democracy is faith in the capacities of human nature; faith in human intelligence and in the power of pooled and cooperative experience.*
>
> —Democracy and Educational Administration, LW 11:219

For reform-minded teachers like myself, no concept of Dewey's is more important than his concept of democracy. I say this because we live in dark times. Increasing globalization, the widening gap between rich and poor, and the escalation of racial, religious, and ethnic hatreds make it difficult to believe that our individual efforts can yield a more humane and equitable future. Loss of hopefulness about the future is especially hard on reform-minded teachers, because the vitality of our classroom practice depends on faith that we and our students can preserve and improve on what is best in our culture.

This is why Dewey's vision of democracy—and his conviction that it is a realistic ideal—is so important at the present time. Dewey's democratic vision balances individual rights and collective responsibilities, seeing every person as entitled to maximum personal growth as long as such growth contributes to respectful, cooperative work with others. Dewey's conviction that his ideal is practicable can help reform-minded teachers regain the hope they need to reinvigorate their classroom work.

Human Nature

On what did Dewey base his optimism that his concept of democracy presented a practicable ideal? In the quote from his 1937 article that is the focus of my short essay, Dewey told us that "faith in the capacities of human nature" is one of the foundations of his concept of democracy. What did he mean? Dewey believed that the "capacities of human nature" may be developed or expressed in manifold ways. That is, human dispositions do not have static or fixed ways of expressing themselves. This approach allowed Dewey to take an optimistic, evolutionary view of human potential, of our powers of imagination and experimentation to develop more caring and equitable forms of association in the future. In other words, we can redesign ourselves.

For example, whether we express our capacity for combativeness by destroying one another or by trying to solve collective problems depends, according to Dewey, on the channels encouraged by our social customs. According to Dewey, these customs can be altered through intelligent, collective action. Viewing our native capacities in this way allowed Dewey to counter those social theorists who were pessimistic about the possibilities of extending democracy, who argued that our combative, self-centered disposition inevitably must lead to oppressive and undemocratic human associations.

At the opening of the 21st century, I believe that Dewey's view is vital for teachers who want to rekindle their hopes for social reform. It can help us find the language and conviction to resist the naysayers who argue that there is nothing anyone can do—not even classroom teachers—to more fully democratize our society.

Intelligence

Dewey's belief that his democratic vision could be realized was based not only on his faith in human nature. It also was based, as he told us in this same 1937 article, on his faith "in human intelligence and in the power of pooled and cooperative experience." This latter confidence rests, in large part, on Dewey's positive view of modern science. As Dewey understood it, the success of the scientific enterprise is the result of shared inquiry and full exchange of information. Modern science exemplifies the social nature of intelligence, the way individual, creative development goes hand-in-hand with participation in shared, collaborative work.

The personal fulfillment and group cooperation that characterize work in the scientific community gave Dewey (and us) a glimpse of the type of relations— the "mode of associated living" (Dewey 1980, 94)—that he saw at the core of democracy, the type of relations that he believed can be practiced by the U.S. community at large.

Cooperative Inquiry

Standing in the way of the full development of more cooperative and democratic societies, according to Dewey, are two factors. The first is the continued use of force and intimidation to resolve our differences rather than the use of intelligent discussion and mutually shaped activity. Dewey wanted us to alter our socially accepted custom of expressing our combativeness by oppressing others and, instead, develop a new custom, one that uses human combativeness for collective good.

The second impediment to a more democratic society is the continued belief that personal happiness lies in the acquisition of material wealth rather than in personal growth generated in cooperation with others. Our belief that our first human need is to compete for material goods conflicts with what Dewey saw as the core value of democracy. For him, the ultimate justification for democracy was the better quality of life that it affords its citizens. For Dewey, democracy provided more opportunities for meaningful experience—more opportunities to be creative and find one's calling—than any other form of associated living.

Vision of Democracy

At first glance, Dewey's democratic vision may seem unrealistically utopian for contemporary classroom teachers because our world has become more focused on competition than cooperation, on material acquisition than creative expression. However, I believe that we can use Dewey's vision—as well as his faith in human nature, intelligence, and cooperative experience—to go against the current, dominant U.S. grain, to go against the idea that democracy is about competing for material goods rather than about developing fulfilling, shared experiences.

In particular, I believe that we can use Dewey's faith to rekindle our hopes that, as teachers, our classrooms can be effective places to plant and nourish seeds of a less competitive and more cooperative ethos. As we encourage students to find their calling, as we develop pedagogies that enable students to practice shared, reflective inquiry, we build upon Dewey's faith in human nature and intelligence. We also keep alive his vision of democracy by contributing, in significant ways, to America's ongoing discussion of its own best future.

References

Dewey, J. 1980. *Democracy and education*. In *John Dewey: The middle works, 1899–1924*, ed. J. A. Boydston, Vol. 9: 1916, 1–402. Carbondale, IL: Southern Illinois University Press.

Dewey, J. 1987. Democracy and educational administration. In *John Dewey: The later works, 1925–1953*, ed. J. A. Boydston, Vol. 11: 1935–1937, 217–25. Carbondale, IL: Southern Illinois University Press.

— ✇ —

Thirty-Eight
John Dewey and the Import of a Curriculum Devoted to Student Experience

Chara Haeussler Bohan

> When nature and society can live in the schoolroom, when the forms
> and tools of learning are subordinated to the substance of experience,
> then shall there be the opportunity for this identification, and culture
> shall be the democratic password.
> —The School and Society, MW 1: 38

In 1900, when John Dewey gave the three lectures that comprise the material for *The School and Society*, lecture and recitation remained a primary method of education (Trenholme 1909). Dewey was not satisfied with such passive learning, and he sought to describe a means of educating students in which they actively participated in their learning through lived experience. He believed that the classroom should be an environment where nature and society happily coexist, rather than a place in which students passively prepare for their future role in the world of work.

Because students engage in life through the use of imagination and develop deeper understandings through lived experiences, Dewey sought to cultivate students' imagination and experiences in the classroom. For students, the Deweyan classroom opened up a world of possibilities.

Considering Students' Interests

Dewey's recommendation to make the methods of learning subordinate to experience has several lessons for teachers in classrooms today. The first is to consider the interests of children and to invest in the learning process by developing activities that can further students' experiences (Tanner 1997). For example, in an elementary classroom where students are to learn basic economic principles, rather than lecturing students and having them only read text, teachers might engage students in an economics fair (Bohan 2003). Students can make a product, earn wages for their labor, and advertise, buy, and sell their products.

In a secondary economics course, students can participate in a classroom activity where they play a game of buying and selling stock on the New York Stock Exchange, and then follow their investments. By considering students' interests and developing a curriculum with experiences to match those interests, teachers necessarily enhance the learning experience. Dewey's attention to experience highlights the difference between learning a foreign language by reading a textbook and learning a foreign language by living in the country where the language is spoken. The latter is a more authentic and effective means of learning.

Arranging the Environment

A second lesson to consider is practical in nature. A teacher must reflect on how the classroom space fosters students' experiences. When Dewey (1976) sought desks and chairs for his laboratory school, he had difficulty finding the proper equipment. He wanted to create an environment in which students could work, rather than simply listen. Similarly, a teacher today must consider the classroom space. The simple task of taking rows of desks and rearranging them in a circle can change the dynamics of student and teacher interaction. As a teacher, standing in the front of the room at a podium lends itself to the lecture format, whereas sitting among the students at a table or in a circle fosters discussion. Some lessons require lecture to convey understanding, particularly to large groups; but other times, actively engaging students to foster dialogue is more prudent.

A teacher ought to be purposeful and careful about how the classroom space is arranged and the type of learning promoted by the physical environment. A welcoming and inviting classroom is a place where learning is easily facilitated. Would a student prefer to read a book in the Magic Tree House series or a classic such as *All Quiet on the Western Front* while sitting on a hard desk chair or in the comfort of a plush and pillowed couch? Students typically spend seven hours of their day in the school environment. Do teachers want students to spend the majority of their day sitting in one position? When the environment presents obstacles rather than offers an invitation, learning is more difficult to accomplish.

Fostering Democratic Character

A third and final component of Dewey's elevation of experience in the learning process is the democratic nature of an education that actively engages students in the world. To foster democratic character in students, Dewey believed, the school had to be organized as a cooperative community (Westbrook 1991). Traditional lecture and recitation demand a more autocratic methodology; but the world of experience requires students to participate in a more democratic form of learning.

Students learn from one another, the world around them, and the projects in which they engage, in addition to seeking assistance from the teacher. When students understand that they are participants in their learning, rather than simply receivers of knowledge, they develop a greater commitment to their education. For students, learning in a democratic environment might mean selecting a topic to research rather than being assigned a research paper.

Dewey's attention to a curriculum based on experience is important to today's teachers and students alike. In an educational world filled with standardized curricula, tests, textbooks, and worksheets, Dewey's philosophy is a gentle reminder about possibilities and ideals in schools where students are the heart of learning. Cultivating students' experiences is a means to promote a lifelong love of learning. Dewey understood the value of a curriculum devoted to student experience.

References

Bohan, C. 2003. A fair to remember: Elementary economics. *Social Studies and the Young Learner* 15(4): 6–8.

Dewey, J. 1976. *The school and society.* In *John Dewey: The middle works, 1899–1924,* ed. J. A. Boydston, Vol. 1: 1899–1901, 1–112. Carbondale, IL: Southern Illinois University Press.

Tanner, L. N. 1997. *Dewey's laboratory school: Lessons for today.* New York: Teachers College Press.

Trenholme, N. M. 1909. The organization of the recitation. *History Teacher's Magazine* 1(4): 74–76.

Westbrook, R. B. 1991. *John Dewey and American democracy.* Ithaca, NY: Cornell University Press.

— ❧ —

Thirty-Nine
The Best and Wisest Parent

David J. Flinders

> *What the best and wisest parent wants for his own child, that must the community want for all of its children. Any other ideal for our schools is narrow and unlovely; acted upon, it destroys our democracy.*
> —The School and Society, MW 1: 5

How do we decide who are the "best and wisest" parents? What makes them best, and what do these parents want for their children? Though Dewey did not take the meaning of "best" parent for granted, at least generally speaking, we might assume that the best and wisest parents watch out for their children's interests and well-being. Such parents want to provide for their children, comfort them, and protect them from harm. But more than this, they want their children to have opportunities to succeed. We might even say that the best parents are those who want the best for their children—including the best health care, the best teachers, and the best education.

Available Resources

Though this initial line of thinking might seem straightforward, we quickly run into some hard economic facts. We live in a society of rich and poor, and the disparity between these groups has grown increasingly wide. Some parents have more resources and more wealth—much more wealth—than others. Their resources allow them to provide more for their children. However, we would not on this basis conclude that all poor parents automatically must be excluded from the "best and wisest" category. By the same token, we would not want to equate "best" simply with being rich. Either way of defining "best" would constitute what Dewey referred to as a "narrow and unlovely" view of parenting.

Individual Needs

Dewey also would caution us on another point; he would argue that any definition is inadequate that attempts to set out the criteria for good parenting without regard for the differences among individual children. Even children who seem alike, such as siblings raised under the same roof, often possess quite different interests, abilities, and aptitudes. Thus, what is best for one child may not be best for others.

The differences among individual children are important in education for the same reason. They raise issues of equity by suggesting that we cannot provide the same course of study for all students without privileging those students whose interests and abilities happen to match the curriculum. Conversely, a one-size-fits-all education would disadvantage those students whose interests and abilities fall outside its scope. Put another way, the best and wisest parents would want each of their children to receive an education matched to his or her individual needs.

Social Criteria

Though Dewey is known for arguing that the needs and interests of children should play a critical role in their education, he did not argue that those needs and interests were the *only* criteria we should consider. Social criteria, for example, are suggested directly in Dewey's references to the vital connections between education and democracy. Dewey's best and wisest parents not only want each of their children to be happy, but they also want them to be acceptable members of the society in which they live. Our culture often pits social and individual concerns against one another; but Dewey saw these concerns as complementary rather than oppositional. It would be difficult, in his view, to raise a self-actualized child who also was entirely unacceptable to a democratic society, or vice versa.

Nowhere is this close integration of social and individual interests more evident than in teaching. In the classroom, as in families, the sacrifice of either interest seriously flaws the entire process. On one side of the issue, we might imagine parents who say, "We love our own children and work hard to provide for them, so why should we be concerned about anyone else's kids?" Or, "Yes, we know many children go hungry and are homeless, but those children are not our problem as long as our own kids are safe and well cared for." We might be sympathetic with what such parents want for their children, and even admire their hard work to provide it. Yet, we should take time to consider their "my child first and only" attitude. This narrow perspective seems uncaring and shortsighted. In what this attitude models or conveys by example, it may fail even the particular children it is meant to serve.

Broad Interest in the World

The care that teachers provide for particular students in their charge involves more than sentimental affection for individual children. It also involves more than helping each child feel special. Rather, caring is reflective work that includes taking a broad interest in the world of which children are a part. Child-centered teachers need not take up social causes directly; but any claim to child-centeredness logically commits them to acknowledging that their own work is something of a social cause.

On the topic of social causes, we might imagine parents fully devoted to various political and philanthropic activities. Perhaps these activist parents are so devoted—as they rush from Habitat for Humanity sites to voter registration tables, to canvassing for Green Peace, to their volunteer jobs at the local humane society—that they have no time left for their own children. Would children be comforted in knowing that such family sacrifice is for noble and worthy causes? If the parents' neglect is genuine, we should be concerned regardless of their otherwise admirable commitments to social betterment.

In the context of teaching, Dewey viewed the needs of the child and the needs of a democracy as serving complementary ends. Schools do not serve democracy, for example, by requiring students to engage in "service learning" against their will. Rather, genuine and lasting social reform involves the nurturing of positive attitudes, abilities, and dispositions. Democratic reform, in short, is more than simply good works. It must also educate people if it is to make a difference. On this count, teachers who say they are reform minded implicitly are committing themselves to child-centered schools.

Reference

Dewey, J. 1976. *The school and society.* In *John Dewey: The middle works, 1899–1924,* ed. J. A. Boydston, Vol. 1: 1899–1901, 1–112. Carbondale, IL: Southern Illinois University Press.

— ∞ —

Forty

The Value of Communication in a Classroom Community

Barbara J. Thayer-Bacon

> *Not only is social life identical with communication, but all communication (and hence all social life) is educative. To be a recipient of a communication is to have an enlarged and changed experience. One shares in what another has thought and felt and in so far, meagerly and amply, has his own attitude modified.*
> —*Democracy and Education*, MW 9: 8

I am sure that when we, as teachers, look at our classrooms full of students, we are able to see that social life exists. Where at least two people are together, there is social life. People who are together in a particular setting at a particular time will communicate with one another in some manner. If they are unable to speak the same language, they will resort to using body language, such as facial expressions and physical posturing, and succeed in establishing some kind of social interaction.

In the classroom, where communication is taking place, there is social life. Even if only two people are in a classroom and they both decide to go to opposite corners of the room and sleep during their time together, they still have communicated something to each other and established a social life. Granted, it is not a very interesting or exciting social life, but all we need is some kind of interaction between at least two people to declare a classroom a place where social life exists.

The Classroom as a Community

When we look again at our classrooms full of students, I wonder whether we can see a community. I believe that a classroom is not only an example of social life; but also is an example of a community—a group of people who have confirmed that they have something in common.

Our students come from diverse contexts, even if our larger school community is ethnically homogenous. We probably have boys and girls, only children, twins, adopted children, children from single-parent homes, widowed-parent homes, and extended-parent homes, as well as students from homes of varying shapes and sizes, with parents of various educational levels or criminal records, just to name a few diverse examples. Given that most towns in the United States today are not ethnically homogenous, our students probably don't all share the same religious and political beliefs, economic or historical backgrounds, or even the same language.

Still, given all that diversity, they share the fact that they attend our class, are exposed to the same curriculum, have you or me as their teacher, and are together as students. I suggest that our classrooms are communities, that there are enough commonalities among individuals to establish some kind of shared experience and shared interest that connects us.

Communicating Shared Experiences and Interests

How does the group of people within our classroom confirm that individuals have shared experiences and interests in common? We do this through communication. If we do not share the same language, then we have to work together to try to learn or create a common language so that we can try to understand one another. If we are lucky enough to share the same language, we don't have to work as hard at finding common terms and establishing common meanings so that we can communicate. However, in spite of sharing the same language, all the diverse backgrounds and experiences we bring to the shared classroom space create many opportunities for us to misunderstand one another. Even in our own homes, miscommunications happen all the time. So why might we think that they wouldn't occur in our classrooms? Of course, they do!

Let's look closer at the challenges of communicating within a diverse classroom community to help us appreciate the educative value of allowing and encouraging communication in our classrooms. When we try to communicate with others, we cannot do so by remaining within our own perspectives. We have to use our imaginations to help us try to think from others' perspectives, to find ways to reach out to them and have our meaning received. We cannot communicate with others by staying within ourselves. We have to get out of our own world view and try to see the world from others' world views.

That effort to reach out allows us to enlarge our thinking. The reaching out we do to communicate is what opens us up to being changed by our communicative efforts. Even if our exchange with others goes smoothly, and there are no misunderstandings, we are changed by the effort we made to reach out to others. And, if our communication does not go smoothly, that creates opportunities for more growth and learning as we try to figure out what went wrong and why. No matter what, we cannot lose; all communication with others leads to growth, and growth leads to education. All communication opens the possibility for us to further our own education as well as the education of others.

Encouraging Communication

The logical conclusion we can draw is that if communication leads to personal growth and education, then we should encourage lots of communication in our classrooms. We should not judge students talking to one another or to us as being "off task" or "wasting time." Instead, we must try to see these communications for what they are—valuable experiences that enlarge our thinking and change us.

I know that teachers are judged in U.S. schools, indeed all over the world, for how quiet their classrooms are. A quiet classroom is a common criterion used for measuring whether or not we are good teachers. Quiet seems to be associated with control, authority, and efficiency, hence more knowledge gained. However, I suggest that our classroom communities need to have many opportunities for communication among members so that we, as teachers, can enhance our students' growth and further their education, as well as our own.

Like Dewey, I encourage you to allow your students more opportunities, not fewer, to communicate with one another and with you in class. Next time you look at your classroom full of students, I hope you will see a place where there is the chance for much growth to take place. Don't be afraid to open up the classroom space to more conversation and discussion. Much learning will take place as a result.

Reference

Dewey, J. 1980. *Democracy and education.* In *John Dewey: The middle works, 1899–1924*, ed. J. A. Boydston, Vol. 9: 1916, 1–402. Carbondale, IL: Southern Illinois University Press.

— ∽ —

Forty-One
The Societal Purpose of Education

Jesse Goodman

> [T]he problem of education in its relation to the direction of social change is all one with the problem of finding out what democracy means in its total range of concrete applications: economic, domestic, international, religious, cultural, and political. . . . The trouble . . . is that we have taken democracy for granted; we have thought and acted as if our forefathers had founded it once and for all. We have forgotten that it has to be enacted anew in every generation, in every year and day, in the living relations of person to person, in all social forms and institutions. Forgetting this . . . we have been negligent in creating a school that should be the constant nurse of democracy.
> —*Education and Social Change*, LW 11: 416

Why do we have public schools? Why should Johnny or Mary or Susie spend hours upon hours in buildings that look like factories but are called schools? On the surface, the question seems innocent—a simple question with an equally simple answer. The question is so rudimentary that most individuals currently concerned about our schools seem not to have noticed it; or perhaps they feel that the answer is so obvious that discussing it would be a waste of time. As most individuals can quickly discern, the design of recent educational reforms has been to help young people get jobs when they grow up. Some people also might add that the function of schools and the recent wave of reforms are meant to ensure our competitive edge over other countries in the global marketplace.

I suggest that our society might benefit from considering Dewey's thoughts on the matter. Specifically, we would achieve much by reopening the debate about the societal purpose of public schooling. Throughout Dewey's life and works, he emphasized two fundamental and closely related purposes for public education. The first might be characterized as a quest for helping individuals create meaning in their lives. The second, as indicated by the quote at the beginning of this essay, is to foster the development of an educated citizenry for the purpose of continually deepening and broadening our democratic society.

The Notion of Public School

Instead of advocating for this or that particular reform, I suggest that what is really needed during these complex times is for us, as a nation, to recast the context within which we debate what should happen in our schools. Rather than situate this discourse within a purely marketplace context, as has been the case for the last decade or so, I propose that we look at public education, as Dewey suggested, within a democratic framework. Let me begin by taking us back to the turn of the century—a time when, as Dewey noted in many of his works, the notion of the public school took on new dimensions.

Though public schools in the United States gradually increased in numbers throughout the 19th century, they subsequently exploded across our country—particularly in our cities—as a result of the massive wave of immigrants that came to live in this land. Thousands of people came to toil in our factories and in the coal mines that produced the energy needed to run a newly electrified society. With these immigrants came their children, and therein was the dilemma. For several years, the prevailing thought was to put these "little beggars" to work alongside their parents; eventually, the cruelty of that existence led to legal prohibitions against that practice. Schools became the solution to the question of what to do with these children, more of whom were coming onto our shores and being born each day.

Teaching Children to Be Good Workers

As schools were built rapidly to keep up with the population explosion taking place in our cities, a debate about the function of these schools began to emerge. Until recently, the debate continued and, at times, thrived in our society. On one side of the issue were those who argued that schools should teach children what they would need to know to be good workers (Bobbitt 1918; Charters 1909; Cubberley 1916). After all, the reason we let these children into our country was because we needed the labor of their parents. It only seemed reasonable that schools should educate these children enough so that they could be even more productive workers than their parents.

Many schools were built with the expectation that the taxpayers' investment would yield a positive return—that is, a more productive workforce. Accordingly, many believed that it was important to teach these children how to speak English; to read, write, and compute math problems; and to follow directions. In addition, there was a call to inform these "dullards," as they were sometimes called (Thorndike 1940), what it means to be an American. Often called civics, this course of study was designed to minimize the value of their traditional ethnic heritages, and to teach these children the innate superiority of our (predominantly masculine, Northern Euro-American) cultural traditions, values, and most importantly governmental and economic institutions. The argument was to drill children until this information and these skills were thoroughly internalized. Sound familiar?

Helping Children Live in a Democracy

On the other side of this debate stood those such as John Dewey (1980) and Boyd Bode (1927) who warned of the dangers embedded in this narrow educational vision. These individuals argued that public schools should be established to help the children of immigrants learn what it means to live in a democracy. Because most immigrants came from societies that were more or less totalitarian and these people often were used to living relatively powerless lives (as victims of economic, social, and ethnic oppression), Dewey argued that we needed schools that could teach children how to thoughtfully participate in not just living in, but also developing a more democratic society.

As the quote at the beginning of this essay stated, Dewey did not want young people to take the democracy that was currently being practiced in our society for granted. To the contrary, he saw room for significant improvements, and he suggested that a truly democratic society never assumes that its democracy is complete. Dewey argued that our schools should help to create a society based not only upon a political democracy, but also a social democracy. Democracy should be thought of as a way of life rather than just the participation of a minority of citizens in a ritual of voting every couple of years.

Ideological Surgery on Our Schools

Throughout the past century, the ideas of Dewey and his colleagues often were overshadowed by those who saw schools as sites for vocational training. However, within the last two decades, this marketplace rationale has so completely dominated the public discourse that the notion of schooling for democracy has vanished from public consideration. Both Democrats and Republicans seem to disagree only on minor details of educational reform with the Bush administration taking this utilitarian orientation toward schooling to new heights.

Unfortunately, many of the most talented teachers and those students who are not academically oriented are being pushed out of our schools (physically or intellectually) at ever increasing rates in Bush's quest to leave no child behind (Aleman et al. 2003; Allington et al. 2003; DeBray et al. 2003; Black et al. 2003; Seashore 2003). The fundamental purpose for schools seems to be taken for granted, regardless of one's political and social values. Americans have been willing to stand by, as if in a trance, while those in power conduct ideological surgery on our schools—cutting them away from any consideration of the relationship between democracy and education, and graphing them onto corporate and military interests (Berliner and Biddle 1995).

Perhaps this surgery has occurred because we have heard so much about the difficulties of economic globalism. However, if educational reform continues to move in its current direction, it is our democracy, not our economy, that will be in peril. One does not have to be a sociologist to recognize that our brand of democracy requires little participation or thoughtfulness on the part of the average individual; and yet the level of even this limited participation is dangerously low. Our national leaders get elected to office in much the same way that soap finds its way into our homes—through slick advertising. We live in an age of sound-bite politics. Instead of engaging in discourses about substantive issues, the focus often degenerates into little more than name calling. Finding out whether someone has slept with someone other than his or her spouse takes on greater significance that one's visions and ideas for the country and the world in which we live.

The quality of the political discussions among our population is worrisome to anyone who treasures democratic values. Though many people blame the politicians or the press for this sorry state of affairs, we—the people of this country—must take ultimate responsibility. Slick advertising, mudslinging, and sound bites all work because, as a nation of citizens, we allow ourselves to be swayed by these substitutes for substantive dialogue. Censorship, racial fears and hatred, poverty, and homelessness are increasing, while values of opportunity for average citizens, authentic compassion, and tolerance for diversity seem to be fading away in many sectors of our society.

The efforts to reform schools in the context of a marketplace rationale have resulted in many new proposals, such as limiting our notion of education to scores students receive on a single, standardized test; legislating that all students must pass this test to graduate; requiring schools to improve the scores on this test annually; the emphasis on phonics, math, and other technical knowledge over more substantive study in the social sciences and humanities; creating student voucher systems; and, most recently, initiating a national curriculum. At the same time, we continue to see children alienated from their studies and teachers who are burned out by all the paperwork required to ensure that Johnny has memorized his daily lessons. All these proposals come at the same time that funding for our schools is being cut and is even more inequitable than when Kozol (1992) called the lopsided funding of our children's education "savage."

What might comprise school reform proposals if the goal was not tied merely to helping children get jobs or to successfully outcompeting other cultures, but rather to making our country a more democratic society in the manner discussed by Dewey? How might schools be funded? What might schools look like if instead of merely trying to raise children's test scores on a single, standardized test that is often given in an atmosphere of anxiety and fear, schools were dedicated to creating educational experiences that would help students become thoughtful, caring, and active participants in the creation of a more democratic culture?

What curriculum might be developed if our goal was to help all children discover their talents, forms of intelligences, and powers of imagination in an effort to make their lives more meaningful? Obviously, the answers to these questions would generate far different visions, ideas, and policy proposals than those being touted by our current government officials.

I am not suggesting that schools should not prepare children for the workplace. After all, every culture has an obligation to educate its young people to participate in the economic activity of the times. However, as Dewey believed, if we are successful in preparing children to thoughtfully take part in improving our democracy, then there would be little need to worry about them acquiring the skills necessary to live in our ever-changing economy. Nor am I suggesting that schooling for democracy would take on one particular form. Dewey did not offer a blueprint. Rather, he simply suggested that if we, as a nation, would begin to discuss the type of education needed to live in a dynamic and socially just democracy, then we would find more viable solutions to the problems that our schools and our society face. Who knows? Perhaps we would once again begin to discuss, as the founders of our nation did long ago, what living in a democracy means.

References

Aleman, E., C. Alexander, E. Fuller, A. Gamoran, J. Hunault, B. Maxcy, S. Mutchler, F. O'Reilly, P. Quiroz, E. Schiller, A. Sobel, J. Warren, and S. Yang. 2003. *Accountability and the politics of education reform.* Paper presented at the Annual Meeting of the American Educational Research Association, April 22, Chicago.

Allington, R., M. Chambliss, R. Croninger, A. Graeber, J. Larson, J. Price, and L. Valli. 2003. *High-stakes accountability and high-quality teaching: Reconcilable or irreconcilable differences?* Paper presented at the Annual Meeting of the American Educational Research Association, April 21, Chicago.

Berliner, D. C., and B. J. Biddle. 1995. *The manufactured crisis: Myths, fraud, and the attack on America's public schools.* Reading, MA: Addison-Wesley.

Black, P., M. Goertz, D. Koretz, and G. Masters. 2003. *Effects of accountability on learning.* Paper presented at the Annual Meeting of the American Educational Research Association, April 22, Chicago.

Bobbitt, F. 1918. *The curriculum.* Boston: Houghton Mifflin.

Bode, B. H. 1927. *Modern educational theories.* New York: Macmillan.

Charters, W. W. 1909. *Methods of teaching: Developed from a functional standpoint.* Chicago: Row, Peterson, & Co.

Cubberley, E. P. 1916. *Public school administration.* Boston: Houghton Mifflin.

DeBray, E., C. Horn, J. Kim, and G. Sunderman. 2003. *The no child left behind education act and its effects on poor and minority students: Findings from the first phase of state-level implementation.* Paper presented at the Annual Meeting of the American Educational Research Association, April 21, Chicago.

Dewey, J. 1980. *Democracy and education.* In *John Dewey: The middle works, 1899–1924,* ed. J. A. Boydston, Vol. 9: 1916, 1–402. Carbondale, IL: Southern Illinois University Press.

Dewey, J. 1987. *Education and social change.* In *John Dewey: The later works, 1925–1953,* ed. J. A. Boydston, Vol. 11: 1935–1937, 408–20. Carbondale, IL: Southern Illinois University Press.

Kozol, J. 1992. *Savage inequalities: Children in America's schools.* New York: Harper Perennial.

Seashore, K. 2003. *Accountability in educational reform: Tensions and dilemmas.* Paper presented at the Annual Meeting of the American Educational Research Association, April 21, Chicago.

Thorndike, E. L. 1940. *Human nature and the social order.* New York: Macmillan.

— ∽ —

Forty-Two
Teaching Our Legislators a Big Idea in 52 Words or Less

Peter S. Hlebowitsh

> *It is the office of the school environment to balance the various elements in the social environment, and to see to it that each individual gets an opportunity to escape from the limitations of the social group in which he was born, and to come into living contact with a broader environment.*
> —Democracy and Education, MW 9: 24–25

Bipartisan support for No Child Left Behind (NCLB) has left many of us in the profession of schooling shaking our heads over yet another small-minded school reform strategy. NCLB has some lively ideas in it, such as referring to the act of reading as a civil right, but its relation to school reform is largely procedural and represents little more than a demand to teach to the test. And its logic is straight out of a Pavlovian experiment gone bad: the public schools either answer the bell by meeting various state-established cut scores on proficiency exams in reading, math, and science or get zapped with a punishment equal to the effect of an electric prod.

Parents who send their kids to neighborhood schools should remember that if one statistically valid subgroup in the school (say, students with disabilities) fails to meet the state cut scores for five consecutive years, the school could become dissolved by NCLB. At that point, the school would be required to recast itself in the form of a charter school or to offer itself over to a private management corporation or a state takeover. And in such a case, almost everyone associated with the school likely would be fired. Even a school's aggregate scores in the 99th percentile (as high as they can be) don't influence this fate. One subgroup out of compliance for five consecutive years, and the school is done in.

The Refrain: Raise the Test Scores

Just think about what our legislators have done here. They finally have found a way to define what a good school does, and they came up with a whopper: good schools raise test scores. The progressive idea of fashioning the school as a comprehensive experience dedicated to socio-civic, academic, vocational, and socio-personal goals (most of which are not easily measured) is largely a lost cause. Raise the test scores is the refrain. And just try to criticize the law as unreasonable, and you're likely to hear someone ask you which child *you* would like to leave behind.

So how did we get such legislation? Some educators, those who lean farthest to the political left, are certain that a right-wing conspiracy is at hand. They believe that a right-wing faction is prepared to dismantle the public schools as we know them, using the annual yearly progress (AYP) data in the NCLB legislation to swing a wrecking ball through the neighborhood school and clear out a spot for privatization efforts. Their case is straightforward. Good neighborhood schools eventually get dissolved, and look who moves into town—the private management corporation rubbing its hands over the prospect of getting schools' access to the public purse.

What a School Does

I, however, am not among the conspiracy theorists. The fact that NCLB is the handiwork of bipartisan cooperation and the states always could tell the feds to get lost makes me think that the law is not moved by anything other than a base misunderstanding of what schools are and what schools do. My theory is that if you can get the legislators to understand the comprehensive agenda of the school, you stand a better chance of getting a comprehensive legislative strategy for its improvement.

Ideally, we could send our legislators back to elementary school, where they could find object lessons in the disconnect between what good teachers do with children and what NCLB tests. But if wishes were horses, beggars would ride. So, I propose something more modest. I'd simply like to ask our legislators to read the 52 words penned by John Dewey in 1916, which precede this essay, and to think about their meaning in the light of NCLB efforts. The intention is to convey a big idea that might encourage a bigger and better view of reform. Here is the quote again (Dewey 1980, 24–25):

> It is the office of the school environment to balance the various elements in the social environment, and to see to it that each individual gets an opportunity to escape from the limitations of the social group in which he was born, and to come into living contact with a broader environment.

To say, as Dewey did, that school provides an experience through which children can escape from the limitations imposed by family and community is quite a mouthful and is quite impolitic today. One could imagine the reflexive criticism from those who might be inclined to portray such a view as anti-family or as going against the core of individuality that makes American democracy so special. I could almost hear it—a Fox news analyst declaring, "And look who the liberals are quoting now: John Dewey, a liberal philosopher who wanted to impose the will of the government on the people and separate them from the very things that the family cherishes most."

So, here is a point that must be confronted. Is Dewey's view anti-family? Most reasonable people will acknowledge that the family is not always a benevolent institution. Ask any teacher, social worker, police officer, or medical doctor, and you're likely to learn a few horror stories about families. Fortunately, however, most parents love their children and take their responsibilities to socialize their children seriously. Parents try to reflect the forms of religion, language, culture, politics, ethics, and so forth that they believe are in the best interests of their children. But this would happen whether there was school in the child's life or not.

The school, on the other hand, doesn't fashion itself along the narrow dimensions of family or neighborhood life. It has a wider normative agenda to build a

141

common experience across the differences that prevail among people, their families, and their neighborhoods. School has to transcend the differences, not by abusing them or ridiculing them, but by offering an expansion of experience that should have some effect in challenging or questioning the parochial.

Building a Common Experience

This is another way of saying that the school has some obligation to widen the margins of experience and to be sure that it finds a way to bring bright ideas about democracy, the problems of living, and history, literature, mathematics, and science into the hearts and minds of children. It also has to cultivate a wide range of skills, including a variety of thinking, inquiry, and communication skills.

Such a project balances the diversifying agenda with the unifying agenda of the school. We unify by teaching a common history, a common language, and common skills and values, as well as by providing a common universe for discourse. We diversify by ensuring that our common experience makes appropriate and useful inclusions of multiple perspectives and by securing a place in the curriculum for individualizing opportunities. Teaching children to read, to do math, and to learn science (the three critical NCLB areas) obviously is important, but so much more needs to be done to ensure that children have the opportunity to escape from the limitations of the experience into which they were born. And such a project will not get done with NCLB standing in its way.

In response to my argument, I imagine that Washington might aim to make NCLB even more pervasive in its testing reach. The logic would be on the scale of saying, "Let's test everything; this way we make everything important." The problem with such a tactic is that no tests designed in the state capitals of our nation could capture the full complement of things that local schools teach children. So, if anything, the approach should move away from a statewide testing accountability system and toward the design of local evaluation systems. If the concern is about accountability, more might be gained if we asked school systems to design comprehensive evaluation systems that were responsive to their articulated purposes and missions (which few schools take seriously today). These evaluations might include tests, but they also might include a variety of other methods or instruments.

This way, the evaluation—including the tests—is of the experience, rather than the reverse. The general idea is to remove the test as a barrier to the fulfillment of the all-inclusive mandate of the school. Doing so would show our legislators that, all things being equal, an idea-oriented school curriculum (even one that yields lower NCLB test scores) that provides cosmopolitan experiences to children is better than a school that provides an impoverished taught-to-the-test experience. That's a big idea—something we need more of in Washington.

Reference

Dewey, J. 1980. *Democracy and education.* In *John Dewey: The middle works, 1899–1924,* ed. J. A. Boydston, Vol. 9: 1916, 1–402. Carbondale, IL: Southern Illinois University Press.

Forty-Three
Collecting and Preserving the Educational Present

Craig Kridel

> *The things in civilization we most prize are not of ourselves. They exist by grace of the doings and sufferings of the continuous human community in which we are a link. Ours is the responsibility of conserving, transmitting, rectifying, and expanding the heritage of values we have received that those who come after us may receive it more solid and secure, more widely accessible and more generously shared than we have received it.*
> —*A Common Faith,* LW 9: 58

I am touched by Dewey's selflessness and his reminder that we are indeed an important part of a larger entity—namely, the continuous human community. We often forget this exulted role as we cope with the constant and endless procession of students who pass through our classrooms. Yet, as Dewey reminded us in his characteristically gentle way, we must not overlook our responsibility to those who come after us.

That ours is to conserve and transmit the heritage of values has become a moral call to me. As a curator of a museum of education, my life is committed to conserving and transmitting the heritage of values that represents our educational system. I maintain that, in what certainly may be construed as an idiosyncratic interpretation of this passage, this same moral call goes out to all educators who live fruitful lives in schools today and who wish to pass on this rich heritage to future generations of teachers and students.

Material Culture and Life in Schools

Why do I raise this topic? Because while much is being written about education—newspaper editorials, professional journal articles, No Child Left Behind critiques, and charter school reports and descriptions—not enough of the material culture of schools is being preserved. *Material culture,* a term commonly used in the fields of archives and museums, refers to those artifacts, documents, and objects modified by humans, consciously or unconsciously, that define and reflect the beliefs and values of the larger society of which they are a part. Can we identify material culture that represents the beliefs and principles that we as educators hold dear for the schools? And, of this material, what is being conserved?

Perhaps various newspaper accounts and journal articles represent your values. Those documents are being saved in our libraries. Further, we can rest assured that federal records also are being kept. The federal government currently generates in a four-month period records equal in volume to those of the first 124 years of our government—from the Washington to Wilson presidencies—all cataloged and archived. Yet, do these federal reports and academic writings truly characterize the heritage of values for which we wish to be remembered?

While this abundant amount of material will survive, does it reflect our lives in schools? Does it embody the markings on a lesson plan (marginalia) for that day when a class finally "gets it"? Does it represent the newsletter clippings with accompanying notes posted by the proud teacher, or the troubled student's corrected worksheet saved by a concerned teacher aide? These are the items, the material culture, that reflect our values and serve to remind future educators that their struggles and their joys of teaching, different yet similar through the years, have been shared by others. The human community of educators is indeed continuous, and it is our responsibility to contemporary times to ensure that our lives in schools are fully documented, solid, secure, and accessible. To this end, I ask educators to accept a role of collecting school culture.

Collecting School Culture

Please do not groan at the thought of yet another educational duty. This role does not require committee meetings, agreed-upon goals and objectives, or even the knowledge of others. The profound gesture of collecting may be an active or sedentary activity with or without a public profile. Further, educators already collect school documents! Today's educational research is filled with the outgrowths of accumulating material culture: teacher portfolio (Bullough and Baughman 1997; Bullough 1989), teacher narrative and autobiography (Clandinin and Connelly 2000; Connelly and Clandinin 1999), portraiture (Lawrence-Lightfoot and Davis 2002), local history (Butchart 1986), and biographical research (Kridel 1998). Teachers compose portfolios for National Board Certification, and students are asked regularly to compile exhibition portfolios of their work. Teacher memoir, narrative, and portraiture have improved staff development and teacher education and, when saved with accompanying artifacts, could transform the presentation and understanding of educational values for future generations.

Could not such school portfolios be prepared for future generations? A scrapbook here and there, a carton of clippings, or one mere filing cabinet drawer in a teacher's room filled with an array of documents and artifacts could more than portray school life for a 10- to 20-year period. The intent is not comprehensiveness; one need not rent storage space at the nearby mini-warehouse. With periodic donations to one's local historical society, a collage of material culture would be preserved. Certainly some teachers would leave such archival treasures, selected with care, as mementos of a rewarding life of teaching.

Preserving the Present

One still may ask whether this preservation is truly necessary. While educational historians talk about the importance of preserving the past, I question whether we are conserving the present. I have spent years assisting researchers who were able to obtain more information about certain classrooms in the 1890s than about educational practices from the 1970s. As I work on a progressive education school study from the 1930s, I find many period documents of students' work and teachers' thoughts and reflections of school life. For some of these same schools, similar materials cannot be located from the early 1980s. Other than a few brochures or yearbooks, little exists. Certain institutions have preserved a distinguished and distinctive past—yet the recent is lost.

Further, the present is being lost during this time that we assume to be an abundant information age. Actually, documents are becoming victims of the false sense of assurance that is suggested with each technological advancement. While paper lasts for decades and vertical files may be accessed by anyone, today's technological storing, arranging, and retrieving of information creates new complications. CD-ROM storage has a life of just 20 years. Audiotapes and videotapes are most likely nonfunctional after as few as 10 years. As computer technology advances, the danger of storing data in irretrievable, antiquated forms increases. I regularly receive e-mail from well-meaning archivists who have found buried material, such as Kaypro files, with no ability to retrieve the records.

Transferring electronic information from one medium to another has been termed *technology refreshing*. I find myself in too many conversations where administrators, far removed from the intricacies of archival retrieval, state how easily the information can be refreshed. However, I rarely hear that funds actually are set aside for such activities. Irreplaceable audiotape cassettes may be digitized and then further refreshed once the DAT (Digital Audio Tape) medium is replaced. But for now, the cassettes wait, playable only until a rewinding snaps and destroys the tape. Many of the Museum of Education's irreplaceable three-quarter-inch Betamax videotape interviews from the mid-1970s remain safe, solid, and secure, yet inaccessible. Perhaps I should be pleased that we were unable to transfer the content to a one-half inch VHS format because we now would be searching for funds to refresh to DVD. Regardless, the irreplaceable content is, in fact, irretrievable.

Even with technology refreshing, many samples of material culture, representing dimensions of school life and the individual lives of teachers, are not conserved. Too often, old technology leads not to refreshing but to dispensing. Many filmstrips and reel-to-reel tapes from the early 1970s are thrown away—not due to bureaucratic inefficiency or to administrative ineptness, but instead to the pretentiousness of living in a technological age where we assume copies abound and always will be preserved—by others.

Preserving with Foresight

Dewey's call, however, should not give carte blanche privileges to anyone to go out and start gathering artifacts. Contemporary materials must be preserved with some foresight. To restate the primordial caveat of archivists: "There is little virtue in mere acquisition if it is divorced from intelligent purpose." I have suffered through too many occasions where a donor has displayed a "willing suspension of significance" and has thrust upon my archives a batch of materials representing little purpose and importance. Material culture consists not of those piles of texts and unused workbooks.

Instead, teacher and student artifacts—corrected worksheets of a child's repeated attempt to complete an assignment, an exhibition poster representing students' work, teacher notes for next week's lessons, meeting agendas with the doodling of a bored staff member, a school newsletter with witticisms (and complaints) jotted in the margins about school policy—these are the items that display the richness of school life. Such perspectives manifest themselves in autobiographies and diaries; in personal narratives and class ethnographies from students' writings and projects; in school and institutional documents, newsletters, annuals, yearbooks, and audio and video documentaries; and in the professional portfolios of education that emerge from our offices as a result of neglecting to prune our filing cabinets. These are the materials, selected from vast unbridled accumulations with the care of a reflective teacher's eye, which must be preserved.

I will be the first to admit that I have interpreted Dewey's statement from *A Common Faith* in a rather peculiar and atypical manner. Yet, his plea to conserve finds its resonance for me in the quest to preserve the educational present and to transmit our educational heritage for those future members of our profession. By accepting an active role in the collection and preservation of educational material culture—*archival agency,* so to speak—today's educators rectify the limiting aspects of lost materials and technological refreshing and fulfill Dewey's plea to expand the heritage of values so that those teachers and students who come after us "may receive it more solid and secure, more widely accessible and more generously shared."

References

Bullough, R. V., Jr. 1989. *First-year teacher: A case study.* New York: Teachers College Press.

Bullough, R. V., Jr., and K. Baughman. 1997. *'First-year teacher' eight years later.* New York: Teachers College Press.

Butchart, R. E. 1986. *Local schools: Exploring their history.* Nashville, TN: American Association for State and Local History.

Clandinin, D. J., and F. M. Connelly. 2000. *Narrative inquiry: Experience and story in qualitative research.* San Francisco: Jossey-Bass.

Connelly, F. M., and D. J. Clandinin, eds. 1999. *Shaping a professional identity: Stories of educational practice.* New York: Teachers College Press.

Dewey, J. 1986. *A common faith.* In *John Dewey: The later works, 1925–1953,* ed. J. A. Boydston, Vol. 9: 1933–1934, 1–60. Carbondale, IL: Southern Illinois University Press.

Kridel, C., ed. 1998. *Writing educational biography.* New York: Garland.

Lawrence-Lightfoot, S., and J. H. Davis. 2002. *The art and science of portraiture.* San Francisco: Jossey-Bass.

— ∽ —

Forty-Four
Education for a Changing World

William Ayers

> *The individual is to be the bearer of civilization; but this involves a remaking of the civilization that he bears.*
> —*The Significance of the Problem of Knowledge*, EW 5: 20

The individual and society are not separate worlds, discreet planets orbiting past one another in infinite space, untouched and unaffecting. No. Individuals are brought forth in a shared space, forever created and shaped in a social surround; every society is constructed, deconstructed, reconstructed at often dizzying speed by actual persons. This is a dynamic, never-ending wheel, spinning and whirring without end. We change the world; the world changes us.

Reaching the Full Measure of Humanity

John Dewey's ideas are as alive and powerful today as ever because he was brilliant, of course, but more because he employed his brilliance in a particular pursuit. Dewey was a dialectician, and he saw teaching as an enterprise geared toward helping every human being reach the full measure of his or her humanity. Education changes lives; education changes the world—simple to say, and yet in countless ways, excruciatingly difficult to enact.

Education, no matter where it is practiced, enables each of us to become more self-consciously human. It embraces as principle and overarching purpose the aspiration that people become more fully human. It impels us toward enlightenment and liberation. And at the center of the whole adventure, students and teachers in their endless variety—energetic and turbulent, struggling, stretching, reaching—come together in classrooms and community centers, a workplace, a house of worship, parks, museums, or someone's home or apartment. They gather in the name of education, assembled in the hope of becoming better, smarter, more capable and powerful, and in the hope of creating a better, more human world. In Paulo Freire's cosmology, this precious, humanistic ideal is an expression of every person's true vocation—*the task of humanization*.

But humanization is not possible in isolation. Rather, it is achieved with others. The dialectical push and pull that Dewey saw so clearly is the engine of personal as well as social growth and change.

In the opening pages of José Saramago's *The Stone Raft* (1995), the Iberian Peninsula, without warning or explanation, breaks free of Europe and begins to drift slowly out to sea. The peninsula migrates east, stops, spins suddenly, and heads south, a kind of large stone raft adrift on an unknown expanse of blue. "You can see where the crack originates," says the narrator, "but no one knows where it ends, just like life itself" (Saramago 1995, 16).

Five strangers are thrust together through a strange set of circumstances, and soon they set off on a voyage of their own. "Don't worry about things making sense," one says. "A journey only makes sense if you finish it, and we're still only half way there, or perhaps only at the beginning, who knows, until your journey on earth has ended I cannot tell you its meaning" (Saramago 1995, 133).

Saramago's stone raft is, of course, also the planet earth, gliding through the fathomless blue, turning and turning around a rather small and insignificant star, charted but not, fated but free, so large that none of us feels like a sailor, so small that we tremble at our insignificance. So many gigantic things lie outside our control, so much seems to just happen to us; it's difficult to take hold of our power and our agency, to make something of it.

Asking Risky and Baffling Questions

We need to learn to ask questions of ourselves and others, to ask risky questions and baffling questions, dynamic questions, and then to live within them—within the contingent answers and the tentative conclusions and the deeper more disturbing questions that emerge. Even when we think of ourselves as open-minded, we are in some large part prisoners of constrained definitions of society, narrow conceptions of human capability. We accept too much.

Perhaps the hardest lesson for all of us to learn is that human identity is not settled, but rather in motion; that reality is not fixed and solid, but dynamic. History is not finished, and we are not living at the point of arrival. People act as if the future is going to be a lot like the present, only more so; but the future is unknown, of course, and also unknowable. Think of any decade in the last century . . . no one could have predicted the changes just ahead, and the impact of those changes on so many aspects of life. Hip-hop. Reality TV. AIDS. E-mail. The atomic bomb. Starbucks. DVDs. Genocide in Rwanda and Bosnia. Knowing this, it is obviously foolish to imagine the future as the present plus, now in spades, and yet our imaginations fail.

"So often we need a whole lifetime in order to change our life," Saramago wrote. "We think a great deal, weigh things up and vacillate, then we go back to the beginning, we think and think, we displace ourselves on the tracks of time with a circular movement, like those clouds of dust, dead leaves, debris, that have no strength for anything more, better by far that we should live in a land of hurricanes" (Saramago 1995, 70).

For better or for worse, we do indeed live in a land of hurricanes, and we ride the crest of a zephyr. Paradoxically, and a little sadly, it is also a land disguised as calm, and we too often experience ourselves as little more than dead leaves and debris.

Living in History

We might cultivate as an article of faith the belief that every human being can exceed where he or she is now—is capable of surpassing himself or herself, of going beyond. One of our challenges, then, is to live and work in the belief that we can do what's never been done, and we might. This requires embracing a most hopeful if scary proposition: we are each, and civilization itself is, a work-in-progress. We are living in history. What we do (or don't do) will make a difference. The outcome is unknown. We act, we doubt, we learn, and we act again.

References

Dewey, J. 1972. *The significance of the problem of knowledge.* In *John Dewey: The early works, 1882–1898,* ed. J. A. Boydston, Vol. 5: 1895–1898, 3–24. Carbondale, IL: Southern Illinois University Press.

Saramago, J. 1995. *The stone raft,* trans. G. Pontiero. New York: Harcourt Brace.

Editors and
Contributors

Editors and Contributors

Editors

Donna Adair Breault is an Assistant Professor of Educational Leadership at Georgia State University where she teaches graduate courses in curriculum, supervision, and organizational theory. Prior to entering higher education, she served as an elementary and middle school teacher and administrator in metropolitan Atlanta, Georgia. Her research involves studying Dewey in the context of curriculum and administration with a special focus on inquiry. She also is interested in promoting public intellectualism among educators.

Rick Breault is an Associate Professor in the Department of Elementary and Early Childhood at Kennesaw State University where he teaches in the undergraduate teacher education program. Earlier in his career, he spent nine years as a teacher in elementary and middle schools in Chicago and Northern Illinois. His research interests include professional development schools, preservice teacher thinking, and church-state tensions in public schools. He is a long-time member of Kappa Delta Pi.

Contributors

Louise Anderson Allen is an Associate Professor of Educational Leadership at Georgia State University. She is the author of *A Bluestocking in Charleston: The Life and Career of Laura Bragg* (University of South Carolina Press 2001) and coauthor of the forthcoming 2nd edition of *Turning Points in Curriculum: A Contemporary American Memoir* (Merrill).

Robert H. Anderson has been a classroom teacher, elementary principal, superintendent of schools, professor at Harvard University, and College of Education dean in Texas. His writings have focused primarily on nongradedness, teaming, clinical supervision, and educational leadership.

William Ayers is a school reform activist, Distinguished Professor of Education, and Senior University Scholar at the University of Illinois at Chicago. His interests focus on the political and cultural contexts of schooling, as well as the meaning and ethical purposes of teachers, students, and families.

Louise M. Berman, who resides in Washington, DC, is Professor Emerita, University of Maryland, College Park. Her field is curriculum studies. Her graduate degrees are from Teachers College, Columbia University, where Dewey's presence had a continuing impact on students and programs.

Chara Haeussler Bohan is an Assistant Professor in the School of Education at Baylor University. Her research interests include education history, social studies education, and women's studies. She is the author of *Go to the Sources: Lucy Maynard Salmon and the Teaching of History* (Peter Lang 2004).

Deron Boyles is an Associate Professor in the Social Foundations of Education program at Georgia State University. His books include *American Education and Corporations: The Free Market Goes to School* (Garland 1998) and *Schools or Markets? Commercialism, Privatization, and School-Business Partnerships* (L. Erlbaum Associates 2005).

Robert V. Bullough, Jr. is Professor of Teacher Education, Brigham Young University, and Emeritus Professor of Educational Studies, University of Utah. Since 1999, he has been CITES Director of Research. Among his publications is *Uncertain Lives: Children of Promise, Teachers of Hope* (Teachers College Press 2001).

Craig A. Cunningham is an Associate Professor in the Department of Integrated Studies in Teaching, Technology, and Inquiry at National-Louis University in Chicago. His research interests include Dewey's metaphysics and theory of moral education, as well as the use of technology to improve teaching and learning.

Marilyn Doerr has been teaching science for more than 25 years, and has taught ecology, chemistry, human anatomy and physiology, and astronomy. Based on experience with her ecology class, she authored *Currere and the Environmental Autobiography: A Phenomenological Approach to the Teaching of Ecology* (Peter Lang 2004).

Elliot W. Eisner is the Lee Jacks Professor of Education and Professor of Art at Stanford University. His work has focused on the arts' contributions to the young's educational development. He is author of *The Arts and the Creation of Mind* (Yale University Press 2002).

Stephen M. Fishman teaches in the Philosophy Department at the University of North Carolina–Charlotte. His study of student learning in his own classroom has resulted in several publications, including *John Dewey and the Challenge of Classroom Practice* (Teachers College Press 1998), coauthored with Lucille McCarthy.

David J. Flinders teaches at Indiana University in the areas of Secondary Education and Curriculum Foundations. His publications include *Responsive Teaching* (with C. A. Bowers, Teachers College Press 1990), *Theory and Concepts in Qualitative Research* (with G. E. Mills, Teachers College Press 1993), and *The Curriculum Studies Reader*, 2nd ed. (with S. J. Thornton, Routledge 2004).

Jim Garrison is a Professor of Philosophy of Education at Virginia Tech in Blacksburg, Virginia. His most recent work is *Teaching, Learning, and Loving* (RoutledgeFalmer 2004), a book he coedited with Daniel Liston. He is a Past President of the Philosophy of Education Society.

Lisa Goeken-Galliart is a sixth-grade teacher in Bloomington-Normal, Illinois, and a part-time instructor in the Curriculum and Instruction Department at Illinois State University.

Jesse Goodman is a Professor of Education and American Studies at Indiana University, Codirector of a master's-level elementary teacher education program, and former Chair of the doctoral Curriculum Studies program. He also is a Codirector of the Harmony Education Center.

James G. Henderson is Professor of Curriculum at Kent State University. He has published seven books on the topics of reflective inquiry in teaching, transformative curriculum leadership, and curriculum wisdom. He is currently Co-editor of the *Journal of Curriculum and Pedagogy*.

Randy Hewitt is an Assistant Professor of Educational Studies at the University of Central Florida. His research interests include pragmatism, critical theory, the reproduction of social class, and democratic education.

Larry A. Hickman is Director of the Center for Dewey Studies and Professor of Philosophy at Southern Illinois University–Carbondale. He is author of *John Dewey's Pragmatic Technology* (Indiana University Press 1990) and editor of *Reading Dewey* (Indiana University Press 1998), *The Essential Dewey* (with Thomas M. Alexander, Indiana University Press 1998), and *The Correspondence of John Dewey*, in three volumes (InteLex 1999, 2001, and 2005).

Peter S. Hlebowitsh is Professor of Curriculum and Instruction at the University of Iowa. He has helped to direct several State Department–sponsored civic education reform projects in Central and Eastern Europe. He is the author of *Designing the School Curriculum* (Pearson 2005).

Tom Kelly is an Associate Professor of Education at John Carroll University where he coordinates the Adolescent and Young Adult Licensure Program. His scholarly interests focus on the meaning, promise, and challenges of critical democratic pedagogy.

M. Frances Klein is Professor Emeritus of the University of Southern California. She has been an educational researcher and frequent presenter at educational conferences. Her research and publication areas include curriculum theory, translating theory into practice, curriculum practices, and classroom practice.

Craig Kridel is Professor of Educational Foundations and Research and Director of the McKissick Museum of Education at the University of South Carolina. He serves on the John Dewey Society Advisory Board. His research interests include progressive education, biography, and documentary editing.

Marcella Kysilka is Professor Emerita, Educational Studies, University of Central Florida. She is Past President of Kappa Delta Pi and former Academic Editor of *The Educational Forum*. Currently, she is a consultant with P.A.C.E. High School, an inner-city charter school in Cincinnati.

Frank E. Marsh is Professor Emeritus and retired Dean of Education at Northeastern University. He was a Ford Foundation Fellow, President of Kappa Delta Pi and Chair of its Educational Foundation for 14 years, and Co-academic Editor of the *Kappa Delta Pi Record*.

Dan Marshall is Professor of Education at Penn State University. As a member of the College of Education's Educational Leadership Program, he teaches courses in curriculum studies and secondary teacher education. His research interests include curriculum studies and various schooling issues.

Robert C. Morris is Professor of Curriculum Studies at the University of West Georgia. He is the Counselor for the College's Omicron Omega Chapter of Kappa Delta Pi. His current research interests are related to leadership activities for curricular and instructional change.

Shelli L. Nafziger, Associate Professor, Coordinator of Elementary Education, and Codirector of the Teacher Education Program at Eureka College, is a doctoral candidate in Curriculum and Instruction at Illinois State University. Her research interests include narrative inquiry, mentoring, and reflection.

George W. Noblit is a Professor and Head of the Ph.D. program in the School of Education, University of North Carolina–Chapel Hill. He specializes in the sociology of knowledge, school reform, critical race studies, anthropology of education, and qualitative research methods.

John M. Novak is Professor of Education at Brock University, St. Catharines, Ontario, Canada. He is President of the Society of Professors of Education. His books include *Inviting Educational Leadership* (Pearson 2002), *Inviting School Success,* 4th ed. (with William W. Purkey, Wadsworth 2005), and *Democratic Teacher Education* (State University of New York Press 1994).

Thomas S. Poetter, Associate Professor of Curriculum in the Department of Educational Leadership at Miami University, is author/coeditor of *Voices of Inquiry in Teacher Education* (L. Erlbaum Associates 1997); *Teacher Leader* (Eye on Education 2001); *In(Ex)clusion: (Re)Visioning the Democratic Ideal* (Educator's International Press 2002); and *Critical Perspectives on the Curriculum of Teacher Education* (University Press of America 2004).

William A. Reid is Visiting Professor of Curriculum and Instruction, University of Texas at Austin. He is author of a number of works on curriculum history and deliberative theory, most recently *Curriculum as Institution and Practice* (L. Erlbaum Associates 1999).

William H. Schubert is Professor of Education and Chair of Curriculum and Instruction at the University of Illinois–Chicago. A former President of the John Dewey Society, he has served as Vice President of the American Educational Research Association and, in 2004, received AERA's Lifetime Achievement Award in Curriculum Studies.

Greg Seals teaches Social Foundations of Education at the College of Staten Island, City University of New York. His main scholarly loves are the metaphysics of education, the philosophy of John Dewey, and school desegregation.

Paul Shaker, who began his career as a humanities teacher, has served as Professor and Dean of Education at six institutions. Currently, he is at Simon Fraser University of British Columbia. As a Fulbright Senior Scholar, he has studied and worked in Japan, Saudi Arabia, and Kuwait.

Edmund C. Short is Professor of Education Emeritus, The Pennsylvania State University, and is currently Faculty Associate, University of Central Florida. He is founding Editor of the *Journal of Curriculum and Supervision* and Editor of *Forms of Curriculum Inquiry* (State University of New York Press 1991).

Daniel Tanner is immediate Past President of the John Dewey Society for the Study of Education and Culture and Professor in the Graduate School of Education, Rutgers University, New Brunswick, New Jersey.

Barbara J. Thayer-Bacon teaches undergraduate and graduate courses on philosophy and history of education, social philosophy, and cultural diversity. Her primary research areas are philosophy of education, pragmatism, feminist theory and pedagogy, and cultural studies in education.

William Van Til, Coffman Distinguished Professor of Education Emeritus at Indiana State University, is author of *The Making of a Modern Educator* (Bobbs-Merrill 1961); *Curriculum: Quest for Relevance,* 2nd ed. (Houghton Mifflin 1974); *Education: A Beginning,* 2nd ed. (Houghton Mifflin 1974); *Secondary Education: School and Community* (Houghton Mifflin 1978); *Writing for Professional Publication,* 2nd ed. (Allyn and Bacon 1986); and *My Way of Looking at It: An Autobiography,* 2nd ed. (Caddo Gap Press 1996).

Gary Weilbacher is an Assistant Professor of Curriculum and Instruction at Illinois State University. He taught middle school for 11 years in Madison, Wisconsin. His research interests include curriculum integration, multicultural education, and youth culture.

Ron W. Wilhelm, Professor in the Department of Teacher Education and Administration at the University of North Texas, teaches courses in multicultural education, curriculum implementation and evaluation, and qualitative research methods. He has served as Counselor for the Alpha Iota Chapter of Kappa Delta Pi since 1992.

George Willis is a Professor of Education at the University of Rhode Island. He has been a member of the Executive Board of the John Dewey Society and a Cochair of the JDS Lectures Commission.

William G. Wraga is Professor and Coordinator of the Program of Educational Administration and Policy, University of Georgia. He teaches and researches in the areas of curriculum theory, development, history, and policy. He is author of *Democracy's High School* (University Press of America 1994).

Transcript of Personal Letter

A handwritten version of this personal letter from John Dewey appears on page 99 of this volume.

My dear Janey and Lucy & Gordon

Your good nice letters came this morning, and as they were written Tuesday you can see how far it is to where I am. This country isn't the mountains, but it is all hills—the funniest kind of hills too. They aren't arranged at all. They just start up everywhere and they are mostly all round so which ever way you go, it is first down & then up, or else first up & then down. The main street is a ridge that only goes down on two sides for a while, but everything else is just knobs & bumps. Maybe ~~Miss Bolli will~~ Gordon will remember Miss Bolli who lived with the Thomases ~~[that over mrs.]~~ the year we lived next to the Thomases.* Well she lives here & yesterday she & her mother took me to drive—a very pretty drive along the river which is lined with bluffs & beautiful hills & woods everywhere. The passion vine was in bloom & grows wild by the side of the road just as woodbine does in the Adirondack.

I am sorry to hear about the wasps; just about 12 years ago there were a lot & Fred & Evelyn took their turns getting "fat" then. I am glad Pine Tree Ledge is still there & I hope it wont slip off downhill before we get back from Europe.

Papa sends you lots of love. Thank Mary for writing for you.

ooooo   xxxxx   +++++
Daddy—

Calvin Thomas and John Dewey were in Ann Arbor at the University of Michigan together.